POWERSHELL PROGRAMMER'S PARADISE: WORKING SMARTER AND FASTER

Microsoft.ACE.OLEDB.12.0 driven HTML coding machine inside!

INSPIRATION: THE DRIVING INGREDIENT

Around this time every year, almost every IT book publisher generates new books in hopes their products will sell. Of course, I'm no different. But with one exception.

You see, I was in your shoes once. I'd purchase any book out there that had even the slightest hint that it would help me perform my job better as a technical support specialist working for Microsoft.

And so, the publishers got my $50 for a book with a page worth of helpful advice that I could share with my customers and, hopefully, that would rachet up my survey percentages and ultimately, put more money in my pocket when those reviews came around.

But I wasn't really impressed with this or the system of publishing books in the first place. Why just give a piece of the puzzle to someone who really needs all the pieces so that that person can be more productive?

And more importantly, what's wrong with making that person more productive?

So, when I got the chance to write the books I wanted to write, I realized I had two problems. One, I am a no name writer producing my own books. The second problem was while I have a lot of knowledge respect to coding in different languages, I had no idea what would work for all my potential readers.

So, I started off with some simple stuff across the different languages to see what would sell and then realized after it was too late to not cover topics that were either already over done or just not what anyone really wanted to purchase.

While easy to write, they were just as easily overlooked and not purchased.

For sure, it was a learning process and took a while before it sunk in that WMI or anything related to it. But add, include or write books about databases and readers were reading and\or buying books.

Which was a good thing because I spent almost all my time at Microsoft covering database related issues and how to make code work using providers, drivers and ISAMS.

In fact, I was so good at solving database related issues that by the time I left Microsoft, I had an 87% satisfaction rating resolving over 3,000 issues.

Still, the urge to put 25 years of journalism experience – I did have a life before Microsoft – was calling for me to start writing about what I knew something about: Automating the process of code so I and, hopefully, you wouldn't have to write the some of the more basic routines again anytime soon.

That's what this book is about: Making the connection using the VBScript interface providing key options that make each PowerShell driven code different and then displaying the output that has been saved to disk – which, these days, is nowhere where you expect it to be. For example. I found the 32-bit versions of the ps1 files in the C:\ directory, the 64-bit files in C:\users\Administrator directory and the HTML files in my C:\users\Administrator directory. Since I'm running a Server OS on my machine, if you are running a client OS just swap out the Administrator to the name of the account you created when you installed the OS. For example, mine would be C:\User\redwar.

Anyway, the program gets rather complex because not only do you have the options to choose the database and the table you want to use, you have the following options:

TableType: Table or Report

Orientation: Multi-Line Horizontal, Multi-Line Vertical (except for Bound), Single-Line Horizontal and Single-Line Vertical

ControlType: None(except for Bound), Button, Checkbox, Combobox(except for bound), Div, Input Button, Label, Listbox (except for Bound), Radio Button, Span, Textarea and Textbox.

Spreadsheets: 14 of them

ADOEngineConfigurations: Connection, Command and Recordset, Connection and Recordset, Command and Recordset, and Recordset

HTMLADOEngineConfigurations: (works only with bound coding conventions) Connection, Command and Recordset, Connection and Recordset, Command and Recordset, and Recordset

Binding Options: Bound, Cloaked, Dynamic and Static.

What all of this adds up to is:

```
3 x 4,928 = 14,784
1 x 9,216 =  9,216
            24,000 unique coding options.
```

What gets me excited is the fact that each one of these coding options averages around 125 lines of code. Meaning, if the average programmer does 65,000 lines of code, getting paid for 2080 hours, that's 31.25 lines of code or roughly 250 lines of code per working day. So, in 30 seconds, you've produced 4 hours-worth of code.

Putting a smile on your face yet?

Well, this fact should: The code you are creating with this program, isn't the real code the end user sees. It is the script needed to produce the output and not the output itself.

From the NWind.mdb, for example, the 10 columns by 77 rows Products table comes out to 1,113 lines. So, if your boss asked you to produce an HTML based report, the physical work is in those 1,113 lines of the actual report and not in the PowerShell script.

In-other-words, you just wrote out a report or table with a stylesheet included that could take a week to do in less than a minute.

I will leave you with that happy thought.

STOP WISHING FOR IT

It is right here

Looking for something you or a friend of yours could use to charge up your new year with a program that works to produce results. Here it is!

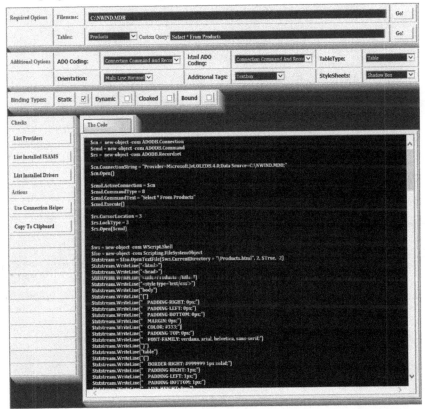

This one uses Microsoft.ACE.OLEDB.12.0 and the code to make it is in this book. So, what does it do?

Purchase the version of this product – past that time – that is in sync with the provider requirements. I have one for each version of the ACE.OLEDB provider up to Microsoft.ACE.OLEDB.15.0.

When you click the first Go button at the very top and right of the program, brings up a common dialog box:

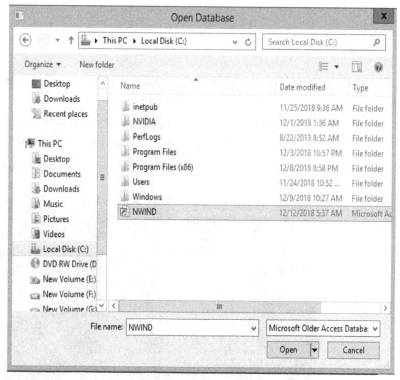

Which I used to connect to an older database file: NWind.mdb. Then Common Dialog filter has an option for both new and old.

Once I have done this, I click the other go button which lists all the tables and views and automates the process of creating creatable queries as seen below:

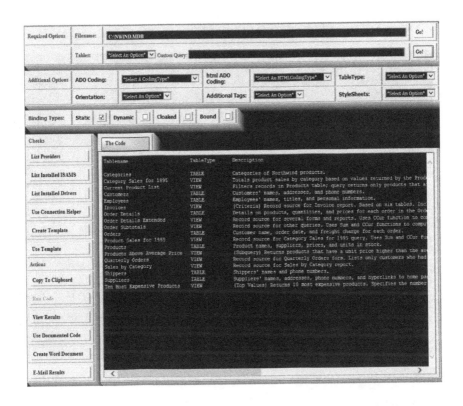

Once I decide which Query to run, because the table type, orientation and control type are set to table, Multi-Line Horizontal and span, respectively html code is generated:

```
$cn = new-object -com ADODB.Connection
$cmd = new-object -com ADODB.Command
$rs = new-object -com ADODB.Recordset

$cn.ConnectionString = "Provider=Microsoft.Jet.OLEDB.4.0;Data Source=C:\NWIND.MDB;"
$cn.Open()

$cmd.ActiveConnection = $cn
$cmd.CommandType = 8
$cmd.CommandText = "Select * From Products" |
$cmd.Execute()

$rs.CursorLocation = 3
$rs.LockType = 3
$rs.Open($cmd)

$ws = new-object -com WScript.Shell
$fso = new-object -com Scripting.FileSystemObject
$txtstream = $fso.OpenTextFile($ws.CurrentDirectory + "\Products.html", 2, $True, -2)
$txtstream.WriteLine("<html>")
$txtstream.WriteLine("<head>")
$txtstream.WriteLine("<title>Products</title>")
$txtstream.WriteLine("<style type='text/css'>")
$txtstream.WriteLine("body")
$txtstream.WriteLine("{")
$txtstream.WriteLine("   PADDING-RIGHT: 0px;")
$txtstream.WriteLine("   PADDING-LEFT: 0px;")
$txtstream.WriteLine("   PADDING-BOTTOM: 0px;")
$txtstream.WriteLine("   MARGIN: 0px;")
$txtstream.WriteLine("   COLOR: #333;")
$txtstream.WriteLine("   PADDING-TOP: 0px;")
$txtstream.WriteLine("   FONT-FAMILY: verdana, arial, helvetica, sans-serif;")
$txtstream.WriteLine("}")
$txtstream.WriteLine("table")
$txtstream.WriteLine("{")
$txtstream.WriteLine("   BORDER-RIGHT: #999999 1px solid;")
$txtstream.WriteLine("   PADDING-RIGHT: 1px;")
$txtstream.WriteLine("   PADDING-LEFT: 1px;")
$txtstream.WriteLine("   PADDING-BOTTOM: 1px;")
```

This is what the code looks like inside the program. Of course, it is a lot clearer in the program than the image shows. At this point, clicking on View Results on the left side of the screen:

ProductID	ProductName	SupplierID	CategoryID	QuantityPerUnit
1	Chai	1	1	10 boxes x 20 bags
2	Chang	1	1	24 - 12 oz bottles
3	Aniseed Syrup	1	2	12 - 550 ml bottles
4	Chef Anton	2	2	48 - 6 oz jars
5	Chef Anton	2	2	36 boxes
6	Grandma	3	2	12 - 8 oz jars
7	Uncle Bob	3	7	12 - 1 lb pkgs.
8	Northwoods Cranberry Sauce	3	2	12 - 12 oz jars
9	Mishi Kobe Niku	4	6	18 - 500 g pkgs.
10	Ikura	4	8	12 - 200 ml jars
11	Queso Cabrales	5	4	1 kg pkg.
12	Queso Manchego La Pastora	5	4	10 - 500 g pkgs.

Of course, how flashy it looks will depend on the stylesheet that you use and the additional tag that you partnered with it.

What is being offered

There is no such thing as a bugless program. Glitches happen. However, the routines – for static, dynamic, cloaked and bound have been tested and work. Additionally, the HTML ADO Coding option, pictured below, only works with the Bound coding option.

You have four basic formats:

Binding Types:	Static	☑	Dynamic	☐	Cloaked	☐	Bound	☐

Each one of these formats allows you to mix Table types: Report or table; Orientation: Multi-Line Horizontal, Multi-Line Vertical, Single-Line Horizontal and Single Line vertical; Additional Tags: Button, Combobox, Div, Listbox, Span, Textarea and Textbox; and 10 style sheets.

THE CODE NEEDED TO MAKE THIS PROGRAM WORK FOR YOU

From below the line is the code you need to create this program:

```
<html xmlns:v="urn:schemas-microsoft-com:vml">
<HEAD>
<HTA:Application
   ID = "Excalibur"
   APPLICATIONNAME = "Excalibur"
   Scroll = "no"
   SINGLEINSTANCE = "No"
   WORKSTATE = "Normal"
>
<head>
<title>Excalibur</title>
<style type='text/css'>
v\:*{ behavior: url(#default#VML);}
body
{
   PADDING-RIGHT: 0px;
   PADDING-LEFT: 0px;
   PADDING-BOTTOM: 0px;
   MARGIN: 0px;
   COLOR: #333;
   PADDING-TOP: 0px;
```

```css
    FONT-FAMILY: verdana, arial, helvetica, sans-serif;
}
Table
{
    BORDER-RIGHT: #999999 1px solid;
    PADDING-RIGHT: 1px;
    PADDING-LEFT: 1px;
    PADDING-BOTTOM: 1px;
    LINE-HEIGHT: 8px;
    PADDING-TOP: 1px;
    BORDER-BOTTOM: #999 1px solid;
    BACKGROUND-COLOR: #eeeeee;
    filter:progid:DXImageTransform.Microsoft.Shadow(color='silver',
Direction=135, Strength=16)
}
th
{
    BORDER-RIGHT: #999999 3px solid;
    PADDING-RIGHT: 6px;
    PADDING-LEFT: 6px;
    FONT-WEIGHT: Bold;
    FONT-SIZE: 14px;
    PADDING-BOTTOM: 6px;
    COLOR: darkred;
    LINE-HEIGHT: 14px;
    PADDING-TOP: 6px;
    BORDER-BOTTOM: #999 1px solid;
    BACKGROUND-COLOR: #eeeeee;
    FONT-FAMILY: font-family: Cambria, serif;
    FONT-SIZE: 12px;
    text-align: left;
    white-Space: nowrap;
}
.th
{
    BORDER-RIGHT: #999999 2px solid;
    PADDING-RIGHT: 6px;
    PADDING-LEFT: 6px;
    FONT-WEIGHT: Bold;
    PADDING-BOTTOM: 6px;
```

```css
    COLOR: black;
    PADDING-TOP: 6px;
    BORDER-BOTTOM: #999 2px solid;
    BACKGROUND-COLOR: #eeeeee;
    FONT-FAMILY: font-family: Cambria, serif;
    FONT-SIZE: 10px;
    text-align: right;
    white-Space: nowrap;
}
td
{
    BORDER-RIGHT: #999999 3px solid;
    PADDING-RIGHT: 6px;
    PADDING-LEFT: 6px;
    FONT-WEIGHT: Normal;
    PADDING-BOTTOM: 6px;
    COLOR: navy;
    LINE-HEIGHT: 14px;
    PADDING-TOP: 6px;
    BORDER-BOTTOM: #999 1px solid;
    BACKGROUND-COLOR: #eeeeee;
    FONT-FAMILY: font-family: Cambria, serif;
    FONT-SIZE: 12px;
    text-align: left;
    white-Space: nowrap;
}
div
{
    BORDER-RIGHT: #999999 3px solid;
    PADDING-RIGHT: 6px;
    PADDING-LEFT: 6px;
    FONT-WEIGHT: Normal;
    PADDING-BOTTOM: 6px;
    COLOR: white;
    PADDING-TOP: 6px;
    BORDER-BOTTOM: #999 1px solid;
    BACKGROUND-COLOR: navy;
    FONT-FAMILY: font-family: Cambria, serif;
    FONT-SIZE: 10px;
    text-align: left;
```

```css
    white-Space: nowrap;
}
span
{
    BORDER-RIGHT: #999999 3px solid;
    PADDING-RIGHT: 3px;
    PADDING-LEFT: 3px;
    FONT-WEIGHT: Normal;
    PADDING-BOTTOM: 3px;
    COLOR: white;
    PADDING-TOP: 3px;
    BORDER-BOTTOM: #999 1px solid;
    BACKGROUND-COLOR: navy;
    FONT-FAMILY: font-family: Cambria, serif;
    FONT-SIZE: 10px;
    text-align: left;
    white-Space: nowrap;
    display: inline-block;
    width: 100%;
}
textarea
{
    BORDER-RIGHT: #999999 3px solid;
    PADDING-RIGHT: 3px;
    PADDING-LEFT: 3px;
    FONT-WEIGHT: Normal;
    PADDING-BOTTOM: 3px;
    COLOR: white;
    PADDING-TOP: 3px;
    BORDER-BOTTOM: #999 1px solid;
    BACKGROUND-COLOR: navy;
    FONT-FAMILY: font-family: Cambria, serif;
    FONT-SIZE: 12px;
    text-align: left;
    width: 100%;
}
select
{
    BORDER-RIGHT: #999999 1px solid;
    PADDING-RIGHT: 1px;
```

```css
    PADDING-LEFT: 1px;
    FONT-WEIGHT: Normal;
    PADDING-BOTTOM: 1px;
    COLOR: white;
    PADDING-TOP: 1px;
    BORDER-BOTTOM: #999 1px solid;
    BACKGROUND-COLOR: navy;
    FONT-FAMILY: Cambria, serif;
    FONT-SIZE: 12px;
    text-align: left;
    white-Space: nowrap;
    width: 450px;
}
select1
{
    BORDER-RIGHT: #999999 1px solid;
    PADDING-RIGHT: 1px;
    PADDING-LEFT: 1px;
    FONT-WEIGHT: Normal;
    PADDING-BOTTOM: 1px;
    COLOR: white;
    PADDING-TOP: 1px;
    BORDER-BOTTOM: #999 1px solid;
    BACKGROUND-COLOR: navy;
    FONT-FAMILY: Cambria, serif;
    FONT-SIZE: 12px;
    text-align: left;
    white-Space: nowrap;
    width: 450px;
}
select2
{
    BORDER-RIGHT: #999999 1px solid;
    PADDING-RIGHT: 1px;
    PADDING-LEFT: 1px;
    FONT-WEIGHT: Normal;
    PADDING-BOTTOM: 1px;
    COLOR: white;
    PADDING-TOP: 1px;
    BORDER-BOTTOM: #999 1px solid;
```

```css
    BACKGROUND-COLOR: navy;
    FONT-FAMILY: Cambria, serif;
    FONT-SIZE: 12px;
    text-align: left;
    white-Space: nowrap;
    width: 450px;
}
#select
{
    BORDER-RIGHT: #999999 1px solid;
    PADDING-RIGHT: 1px;
    PADDING-LEFT: 1px;
    FONT-WEIGHT: Normal;
    PADDING-BOTTOM: 1px;
    COLOR: white;
    PADDING-TOP: 1px;
    BORDER-BOTTOM: #999 1px solid;
    BACKGROUND-COLOR: navy;
    FONT-FAMILY: Cambria, serif;
    FONT-SIZE: 12px;
    text-align: left;
    white-Space: nowrap;
    width: 100px;
}
select4
{
    BORDER-RIGHT: #999999 1px solid;
    PADDING-RIGHT: 1px;
    PADDING-LEFT: 1px;
    FONT-WEIGHT: Normal;
    PADDING-BOTTOM: 1px;
    COLOR: white;
    PADDING-TOP: 1px;
    BORDER-BOTTOM: #999 1px solid;
    BACKGROUND-COLOR: navy;
    FONT-FAMILY: Cambria, serif;
    FONT-SIZE: 12px;
    text-align: left;
    white-Space: nowrap;
    width: 254px;
```

```
    }
    input
    {
       BORDER-RIGHT: #999999 3px solid;
       PADDING-RIGHT: 3px;
       PADDING-LEFT: 3px;
       FONT-WEIGHT: Bold;
       PADDING-BOTTOM: 3px;
       COLOR: white;
       PADDING-TOP: 3px;
       BORDER-BOTTOM: #999 1px solid;
       BACKGROUND-COLOR: navy;
       FONT-FAMILY: font-family: Cambria, serif;
       FONT-SIZE: 12px;
       text-align: left;
       display: table-cell;
       white-Space: nowrap;
       width: 100%;
    }
    </style>
    <body BGColor=#242424>
    <table          style="Position:Absolute;Top:0px;Left:0px;Width:900px;Font-
family:Tahoma;font-size:10px">
    <tr><th   class=tdbackground   align=Right   Width=100px   nowrap>Required
Options</th>
    <th align=right style="Width:77px;" nowrap><b>Filename:</b></th>
    <td   align=left   nowrap><input   Type='text'   id='FName'   name='FName'
style='width:750px;'></input></td>
    <td><input         Type='Button'         id='Search'         name='Search'
style='width:50px;Background-color:ButtonFace;color:black;'
Value="Go!"></input></td>
    </tr>
    <tr>
    <tr><th class=tdbackground align=Right Width=115px nowrap> </th>
    <th align=right Width=77px nowrap><b>Tables: </b></th>
    <td   align=left   nowrap><select   id="trex"   style="width:125px;background-
Color:navy;Color:White;"               onChange="HandlestrexChange()"
name="trexPullDown"></select>
    Custom   Query: <input   Type='text'   id='CQuery'   name=CQuery'
style='width:540px;'></input>
```

```html
        </td>
        <td><input Type='Button' id='LT1' name='LT1' style='width:50px;Background-color:ButtonFace;color:black;' Value="Go!"></input></td></tr>
    </table>


    <table          style="Position:Absolute;Top:100px;Left:0px;Width:900px;Font-family:Tahoma;font-size:10px">
    <tr><th class=tdbackground align=Center nowrap>Additional Options</th>
    <th        class="myclass"          Style="color:Black;font-family:Tahoma;font-size:12px;width:115px;" Align=Right Nowrap>ADO Coding:</TH>
    <th><SELECT              ID="ADOCoding"                 class="myclass1"
style="width:195px;background-Color:navy;Color:White"
onChange="HandlesEngineTypeChange()" name="EngineTypePullDown">
    <option Value="*Select A CodingType*">*Select A CodingType*</option>
    <option Value="cncmdrs">Connection Command And Recordset</option>
    <option Value="cnrs">Connection And Recordset</option>
    <option Value="cmdrs">Command And Recordset</option>
    <option Value="rs">Recordset</option>
    </SELECT></th>
    <th         class="myclass"          Style="color:Black;font-family:Tahoma;font-size:12px;width:115px;" Align=Right Nowrap>html ADO Coding:</TH>
    <th><SELECT              ID="HTMLADOCoding"              class="myclass1"
style="width:195px;background-Color:navy;Color:White"
onChange="HandlesHTMLEngineTypeChange()"
name="HTMLEngineTypePullDown">
    <option       Value="*Select     An      HTMLCodingType*">*Select       An
HTMLCodingType*</option>
    <option Value="cncmdrs">Connection Command And Recordset</option>
    <option Value="cnrs">Connection And Recordset</option>
    <option Value="cmdrs">Command And Recordset</option>
    <option Value="rs">Recordset</option>
    </SELECT></th>
    <th         class="myclass"          Style="color:Black;font-family:Tahoma;font-size:12px;width:115px;" Align=Right Nowrap>TableType:</TH>
    <th><SELECT              ID="TableType"                 class="myclass1"
style="width:125px;background-Color:navy;Color:White"
onChange="HandlesTableTypeChange()" name="TableTypePullDown">
    <option Value="*Select A TableType*">*Select An Option*</option>
    <option Value="Table">Table</option>
    <option Value="Report">Report</option>
```

```
</SELECT></th>
</tr>
<tr>
<th class=tdbackground align=Center nowrap> </th><th class="myclass"
Style="color:Black;font-family:Tahoma;font-size:12px"    Align=Right       nowrap>
Orientation:</TH>
<th>
<SELECT              class="myclass1"                   style="width:125px;background-
Color:navy;Color:White"                   onChange="HandlesOrientationChange()"
name="OrientationPullDown">
<option selected Value="*Select An Orientation*">*Select An Option*</option>
<option Value="Multi-Line Horizontal">Multi-Line Horizontal</option>
<option Value="Multi-Line Vertical">Multi-Line Vertical</option>
<option Value="Single-Line Horizontal">Single-Line Horizontal</option>
<option Value="Single-Line Vertical">Single-Line Vertical</option>
</SELECT></TH>
<TH   class="myclass"   Style="color:Black;font-family:Tahoma;font-size:12px"
Align=Right nowrap>    Additional Tags:</TH>
<TH>
<SELECT              class="myclass1"                   style="width:125px;background-
Color:navy;Color:White"                   onChange="HandlesControlTypeChange()"
name="ControlTypePullDown">
<option    selected   Value="*Select   An   Additional   Tag*">*Select   An
Option*</option>
<option Value="Button">Button</option>
<option Value="Checkbox">Checkbox</option>
<option Value="Combobox">Combobox</option>
<option Value="Div">Div</option>
<option Value="Input Button">Input Button</option>
<option Value="Label">Label</option>
<option Value="Listbox">Listbox</option>
<option Value="Radio Button">Radio Button</option>
<option Value="Span">Span</option>
<option Value="Textarea">Textarea</option>
<option Value="Textbox">Textbox</option>
</SELECT></TH>
<TH   class="myclass"   Style="color:Black;font-family:Tahoma;font-size:12px"
Align=Right nowrap>    StyleSheets:</TH>
<TH>
```

```
<SELECT                 class="myclass"                 style="width:125px;background-
Color:navy;Color:White"                 onChange="HandlesStyleSheetChange()"
name="StyleSheetPullDown">
  <option selected Value="*Select A StyleSheet*">*Select An Option*</option>
  <option Value="None">None</option>
  <option Value="Basic">Basic</option>
  <option Value="InLine">InLine</option>
  <option Value="BlackAndWhiteText">Black And White Text</option>
  <option Value="OscillatingRowColors">Oscillating Row Colors</option>
  <option Value="ColoredText">Colored Text</option>
  <option Value="GhostDecorated">Ghost Decorated</Option>
  <option Value="3D">3d</option>
  <option Value="ShadowBox">Shadow Box</option>
  <option Value="Customized">Customized</options>
  </select></TH></TR>
  </table>
  <table                 style="Position:Absolute;Top:190px;Left:0px;Width:400px;Font-
family:Tahoma;font-size:10px">
  <tr><th                      class="myclass"                      Style="background-
Color:buttonface;color:darkred;font-family:Tahoma;font-size:12px;Width:115px"
Align=Right nowrap>Binding Types:</th>
  <th  Style="background-Color:buttonface;color:Black;font-family:Tahoma;font-
size:12px" Align=Right nowrap>Static</th>
  <th><input       type='checkbox'       id='st'       name='st'       checked=true
style="width:25px;background-Color:buttonface;Color:black"></input></th>
  <th  Style="background-Color:buttonface;color:Black;font-family:Tahoma;font-
size:12px" Align=Right nowrap>Dynamic</th>
  <th><input           type='checkbox'           id='dynamic'           name='dynamic'
style="width:25px;background-Color:buttonface;Color:black"></input></th>
  <th  Style="background-Color:buttonface;color:Black;font-family:Tahoma;font-
size:12px" Align=Right nowrap>Cloaked</th>
  <th><input           type='checkbox'           id='cloaked'           name='cloaked'
style="width:25px;background-Color:buttonface;Color:black"></input></th>
  <th  Style="background-Color:buttonface;color:Black;font-family:Tahoma;font-
size:12px" Align=Right nowrap>Bound</th>
  <th><input           type='checkbox'           id='bound'           name='bound'
style="width:25px;background-Color:buttonface;Color:black"></input></th>
  </tr>
  </table>
```

```html
<table style="Position:Absolute;Top:245px;Left:0px;Font-family:Tahoma;font-size:10px">
<TR><TH class=td background align=Center nowrap colspan=6>Checks</TH></TR>
<TR>
<TH align=left nowrap>
<input Type='Button' id='Providers' name='Providers' style='width:150px;Background-color:ButtonFace;color:black;' Value="List Providers"></input>
</TH></TR>
<TR>
<TH align=left nowrap>
<input Type='Button' id='ISAMS' name='ISAMS' style='width:150px;Background-color:ButtonFace;color:black;' Value="List Installed ISAMS"></input>
</TH></TR>
<TR>
<TH align=left nowrap">
<input Type='Button' id='Drivers' name='Drivers' style='width:150px;Background-color:ButtonFace;color:black;' Value="List Installed Drivers"></input>
</th></tr>
<TR>
<TR><TH class=td background align=Center nowrap colspan=5>Actions</TH></TR>
<tr>
<TH align=left nowrap>
<input Type='Button' id='DataLinks1' name='DataLinks1' style='width:150px;Background-color:ButtonFace;color:black;' Value="Use Connection Helper"></input>
</TH></TR>
<TR>
<TH align=left nowrap">
<input Type='Button' id='Clipboard1' name='Clipboard1' style='width:150px;Background-color:ButtonFace;color:black;' Value="Copy To Clipboard"></input>
</TH></TR>
<tr>
<TH align=left nowrap> </TH></TR>
<tr>
```

```
<TH align=left nowrap> </TH></TR>
<tr>
<TH align=left nowrap> </TH></TR>
<tr>
<TH align=left nowrap> </TH></TR>
<tr>
<TH align=left nowrap> </TH></TR>
<TR>
<TH align=left nowrap> </TH></TR>
<TR>
<TH align=left nowrap> </TH></TR>
<TR>
<TH align=left nowrap> </TH></TR>
<TR>
<TH align=left nowrap> </TH></TR>
<tr>
<TH align=left nowrap> </TH></TR>
<TR>
<TH align=left nowrap> </TH></TR>
</table>


<TABLE                    style="Position:Absolute;Top:245px;Left:180px;Font-
family:Tahoma;font-size:10px">
<TR><TH>
    <v:roundrect id="A" style="width:120;height:30px" arcsize="5%">
    <v:fill   color="#CCCCCC"   color2="white"   Opacity=90%      Opacity2=90%
method="linear sigma" angle="-135" type="gradientradial" />
    <v:textbox          id="A1"              style="font-family:Garmond;Font-
size:12px;Color:darkred"><b>The Code</b></v:textbox>
    <v:shadow   id="A2"   on="false"   offset="3pt,   3pt"   opacity="70%"
color="black"/>
    </v:roundrect>
  </TH></TR>
  </TABLE>


<TABLE                    style="border:solid;border-color:Blue;border-
width:1px;Position:Absolute;Left:180;Top:285px;width:832px;Height:595px">
<TR><TH>
```

```
<Textarea    ID="Textarea1"    name="Textarea1"    style='background-
Color:#000033;font-family:    Cambria,    serif;font-weight:bold;font-
size:12px;Height:590px;Width:832px;' wrap="off"></textarea></TH></TR>
</TABLE>


<script language="vbscript">

Dim cnstr
Dim cn
Dim Provider
Dim rs

Dim EngineConfiguration
Dim HTMLEngineConfiguration
Dim txtstream
Dim TableType
Dim Orientation
Dim ControlType
Dim Filename
Dim strQuery
Dim Tablename
Dim Value
Dim StyleSheet


Provider="Microsoft.ACE.OLEDB.12.0"

Filename = ""
strQuery = ""
Tablename = ""

EngineConfiguration = "rs"
HTMLEngineConfiguration = "rs"
TableType = "Table"
Orientation = "Multi-Line Horizontal"
ControlType = "Span"
StyleSheet = "InLine"

Sub Window_onLoad()
```

```
        window.moveTo 0, 0
        window.resizeTo 1055, 975

    End Sub

    Sub HandlesEngineTypeChange()

        If EngineTypePullDown.Value <> "*Select An Option*" then

            EngineConfiguration = EngineTypePullDown.Value

        End If

    End sub

    Sub HandlesHTMLEngineTypeChange()

        If HTMLEngineTypePullDown.Value <> "*Select An Option*" then

            HTMLEngineConfiguration = HTMLEngineTypePullDown.Value

        End If

    End sub

Sub st_OnClick()
    If st.Checked = true then
        dynamic.Checked = false
        cloaked.Checked = false
        bound.Checked = false
        If trexPullDown.Value <> "*Select An Option*" then
            Write_The_Code
        End If
    End If
End Sub

Sub dynamic_OnClick()
    If dynamic.Checked = true then
        st.Checked = false
```

```
          cloaked.Checked = false
          bound.Checked = false
          If trexPullDown.Value <> "*Select An Option*" then
             Write_The_Code
          End If
       End If
     End Sub


     Sub cloaked_OnClick()
       If cloaked.Checked = true then
          dynamic.Checked = false
          st.Checked = false
          bound.Checked = false
          If trexPullDown.Value <> "*Select An Option*" then
             Write_The_Code
          End If
       End If
     End Sub


     Sub bound_OnClick()
       If bound.Checked = true then
          dynamic.Checked = false
          cloaked.Checked = false
          st.Checked = false
          If trexPullDown.Value <> "*Select An Option*" then
             Write_The_Code
          End If
       End If
     End Sub



     Sub HandlesTableTypeChange()

        If TableTypePullDown.Value <> "*Select A TableType*" Then
           TableType = TableTypePullDown.Value
           Write_The_Code

        End If

     End Sub
```

```vb
Sub HandlestrexChange()

    If trexPullDown.Value <> "*Select An Option*" then

        dim pos
        pos = instr(trexPullDown.Value, " ")
        if pos > 0 then
            CQuery.Value = "Select * From [" + trexPullDown.Value + "]"
        else
            CQuery.Value = "Select * From " + trexPullDown.Value
        End If

    End If

End Sub


Sub HandlesOrientationChange()

    If OrientationPullDown.Value <> "*Select An Orientation*" Then
        Orientation = OrientationPullDown.Value
        Write_The_Code
    End If

End Sub

Sub HandlesControlTypeChange()

    If ControlTypePullDown.Value <> "*Select An Additional Tag*" Then
        ControlType = ControlTypePullDown.Value
        Write_The_Code
    End If

End Sub

Sub HandlesStyleSheetChange()

If StyleSheetPullDown.Value <> "*Select A StyleSheet*" Then
```

```
        StyleSheet = StyleSheetPullDown.Value
        Write_The_Code
    End If

End Sub

Sub Write_The_Code()

    textarea1.innerText = ""

    If FName.Value = "" then
        msgbox("Please provide the location and name of the database you want
to use before clicking here.")
        exit sub
    else
        Filename = FName.Value
    End If

    If CQuery.Value = "" then
        msgbox("Please create a Query string before clicking here.")
        exit sub
    End If

    strQuery = CQuery.Value

    dim pos
    pos = instr(trexPullDown.Value, " ")
    if pos > 0 then
        Tablename = Replace(trexPullDown.Value, " ", "_")
    else
        Tablename = trexPullDown.Value
    End If

    Initialize_File_Creation
    Initialize_Data_Engine_Configuration

    if st.Checked = True then
        Do_Static
        Write_The_Happy_Ending
        Exit Sub
```

```
End If

if dynamic.Checked = True then

    Do_Dynamic
    Write_The_Happy_Ending
    Exit Sub

End If

if cloaked.Checked = True then

    Do_Cloaked
    Write_The_Happy_Ending
    Exit Sub

End If

if bound.Checked = True then

    Do_Bound
    Write_The_Happy_Ending
    Exit Sub

End If



End sub


Sub Initialize_File_Creation()

    Set ws = CreateObject("WScript.Shell")
    Set fso = CreateObject("Scripting.FileSystemObject")
    Set txtstream = fso.OpenTextFile(ws.CurrentDirectory + "\" + Tablename +
".ps1", 2, True, -2)

    End Sub
```

```
Sub Initialize_Data_Engine_Configuration()

    Select Case EngineConfiguration


        Case "cncmdrs"

                txtstream.WriteLine("   $cn = new-object -com ADODB.Connection ")
                txtstream.WriteLine("   $cmd = new-object -com ADODB.Command ")
                txtstream.WriteLine("   $rs = new-object -com ADODB.Recordset ")
                txtstream.WriteLine("")
                txtstream.WriteLine("          $cn.ConnectionString = ""Provider="  +
Provider + ";Data Source=" + fName.Value + ";"" ")
                txtstream.WriteLine("   $cn.Open()")
                txtstream.WriteLine("")
                txtstream.WriteLine("   $cmd.ActiveConnection = $cn")
                txtstream.WriteLine("   $cmd.CommandType = 8")
                txtstream.WriteLine("   $cmd.CommandText = """" + strQuery + """" ")
                txtstream.WriteLine("   $cmd.Execute()")
                txtstream.WriteLine("")
                txtstream.WriteLine("   $rs.CursorLocation = 3")
                txtstream.WriteLine("   $rs.LockType = 3")
                txtstream.WriteLine("   $rs.Open($cmd)")
                txtstream.WriteLine("")

        Case "cnrs"

                txtstream.WriteLine("   $cn = new-object -com ADODB.Connection ")
                txtstream.WriteLine("   $rs = new-object -com ADODB.Recordset ")
                txtstream.WriteLine("")
                txtstream.WriteLine("          $cn.ConnectionString = ""Provider="  +
Provider + ";Data Source=" + fName.Value + ";"" ")
                txtstream.WriteLine("   $cn.Open()")
                txtstream.WriteLine("")
                txtstream.WriteLine("   $rs.ActiveConnection = $cn")
                txtstream.WriteLine("   $rs.CursorLocation = 3")
                txtstream.WriteLine("   $rs.LockType = 3")
                txtstream.WriteLine("   $rs.Source = """" + strQuery + """" ")
                txtstream.WriteLine("   $rs.Open()")
```

```
        Case "cmdrs"

                txtstream.WriteLine("   $cmd = new-object -com ADODB.Command ")
                txtstream.WriteLine("   $rs = new-object -com ADODB.Recordset ")
                txtstream.WriteLine("        $cmd.ActiveConnection = ""Provider=" +
Provider + ";Data Source=" + fName.Value + ";""" ")
                txtstream.WriteLine("   $cmd.CommandType = 8")
                txtstream.WriteLine("   $cmd.CommandText = """" + strQuery + """" ")
                txtstream.WriteLine("   $cmd.Execute()")
                txtstream.WriteLine("")
                txtstream.WriteLine("   $rs.CursorLocation = 3")
                txtstream.WriteLine("   $rs.LockType = 3")
                txtstream.WriteLine("   $rs.Open($cmd)")
                txtstream.WriteLine("")

        Case "rs"

                txtstream.WriteLine("   $rs = new-object -com ADODB.Recordset ")
                txtstream.WriteLine("   $rs.ActiveConnection = ""Provider=" + Provider +
";Data Source=" + fName.Value + ";""" ")
                txtstream.WriteLine("   $rs.LockType = 3")
                txtstream.WriteLine("   $rs.Cursorlocation = 3")
                txtstream.WriteLine("   $rs.Source = """" + strQuery + """" ")
                txtstream.WriteLine("   $rs.Open()")
                txtstream.WriteLine("")

        End Select


        txtstream.WriteLine("")



        txtstream.WriteLine("   $ws = new-object -com WScript.Shell ")
        txtstream.WriteLine("   $fso = new-object -com Scripting.FileSystemObject ")
        txtstream.WriteLine("   $txtstream = $fso.OpenTextFile($ws.CurrentDirectory
+ """\" + Tablename + ".html""", 2, $True, -2)")
        txtstream.WriteLine("   $txtstream.WriteLine(""<html>"")")
        txtstream.WriteLine("   $txtstream.WriteLine(""<head>"")")
```

```
txtstream.WriteLine("        $txtstream.WriteLine(""""<title>" + Tablename + "</title>"""")")

Add_The_StyleSheet


If Bound.Checked = true then

    Select Case HTMLEngineConfiguration


        Case "cncmdrs"

            txtstream.WriteLine("                        $txtstream.WriteLine(""""<object id="""""""cmd"""""""             CLASSID="""""""clsid:00000507-0000-0010-8000-00AA006D2EA4""""""" height="""""""0""""""" width="""""""0"""""""></object>"""")")
            txtstream.WriteLine("                        $txtstream.WriteLine(""""<object id="""""""cn"""""""             CLASSID="""""""clsid:00000514-0000-0010-8000-00AA006D2EA4""""""" height="""""""0""""""" width="""""""0"""""""></object>"""")")
            txtstream.WriteLine("                        $txtstream.WriteLine(""""<object id="""""""rs"""""""             CLASSID="""""""clsid:00000535-0000-0010-8000-00AA006D2EA4""""""" height="""""""0""""""" width="""""""0"""""""></object>"""")")
            txtstream.WriteLine("   $txtstream.WriteLine(""""</head>"""")")
            txtstream.WriteLine("   $txtstream.WriteLine(""""<body>"""")")
            txtstream.WriteLine("                        $txtstream.WriteLine(""""<script language='vbscript'>"""")")
            txtstream.WriteLine("   $txtstream.WriteLine("""""""") ")
            txtstream.WriteLine("   $txtstream.WriteLine(""""cn.ConnectionString = """""""Provider=" + Provider + ";Data Source=" + fName.Value + ";""""""" """")")
            txtstream.WriteLine("   $txtstream.WriteLine(""""Call cn.Open"""")")
            txtstream.WriteLine("   $txtstream.WriteLine("""""""") ")
            txtstream.WriteLine("   $txtstream.WriteLine(""""cmd.ActiveConnection = cn"""")")
            txtstream.WriteLine("   $txtstream.WriteLine(""""cmd.CommandType = 8"""")")
            txtstream.WriteLine("   $txtstream.WriteLine(""""cmd.CommandText = """""""""" + strQuery + """""""""" """")")
            txtstream.WriteLine("   $txtstream.WriteLine(""""Call cmd.Execute"""")")
            txtstream.WriteLine("   $txtstream.WriteLine("""""""") ")
```

```
                txtstream.WriteLine("        $txtstream.WriteLine(""rs.CursorLocation =
3"")")
                txtstream.WriteLine("    $txtstream.WriteLine(""rs.LockType = 3"")")
                txtstream.WriteLine("                    $txtstream.WriteLine(""Call
rs.Open(cmd)"")")
                txtstream.WriteLine("   $txtstream.WriteLine("""") ")
                txtstream.WriteLine("                    $txtstream.WriteLine(Chr(60)    +
""/script>"")")

        Case "cnrs"

                txtstream.WriteLine("                    $txtstream.WriteLine(""<object
id=""""""cn""""""            CLASSID=""""""clsid:00000514-0000-0010-8000-
00AA006D2EA4"""""" height=""""""0"""""" width=""""""0""""""></object>"")")
                txtstream.WriteLine("                    $txtstream.WriteLine(""<object
id=""""""rs""""""            CLASSID=""""""clsid:00000535-0000-0010-8000-
00AA006D2EA4"""""" height=""""""0"""""" width=""""""0""""""></object>"")")
                txtstream.WriteLine("   $txtstream.WriteLine(""</head>"")")
                txtstream.WriteLine("   $txtstream.WriteLine(""<body>"")")
                txtstream.WriteLine("                    $txtstream.WriteLine(""<script
language='vbscript'>"")")
                txtstream.WriteLine("   $txtstream.WriteLine("""") ")
                txtstream.WriteLine("   $txtstream.WriteLine(""cn.ConnectionString =
""""""Provider=" + Provider + ";Data Source=" + fName.Value + ";"""""" "")")
                txtstream.WriteLine("   $txtstream.WriteLine(""Call cn.Open"")")
                txtstream.WriteLine("   $txtstream.WriteLine("""") ")
                txtstream.WriteLine("   $txtstream.WriteLine(""rs.ActiveConnection =
cn"") ")
                txtstream.WriteLine("        $txtstream.WriteLine(""rs.CursorLocation =
3"")")
                txtstream.WriteLine("   $txtstream.WriteLine(""rs.LockType = 3"")")
                txtstream.WriteLine("   $txtstream.WriteLine(""rs.Source = """""""" +
strQuery + """""""" "")")
                txtstream.WriteLine("   $txtstream.WriteLine(""call rs.Open()"")")
                txtstream.WriteLine("   $txtstream.WriteLine("""") ")
                txtstream.WriteLine("                    $txtstream.WriteLine(Chr(60)    +
""/script>"")")

        Case "cmdrs"
```

```vbscript
              txtstream.WriteLine("                    $txtstream.WriteLine(""""<object
id="""""""cmd"""""""                    CLASSID="""""""clsid:00000507-0000-0010-8000-
00AA006D2EA4"""""""" height="""""""0"""""""" width="""""""0""""""""></object>"""")")
              txtstream.WriteLine("                    $txtstream.WriteLine(""""<object
id="""""""rs"""""""                    CLASSID="""""""clsid:00000535-0000-0010-8000-
00AA006D2EA4"""""""" height="""""""0"""""""" width="""""""0""""""""></object>"""")")
              txtstream.WriteLine("    $txtstream.WriteLine(""""</head>"""")")
              txtstream.WriteLine("    $txtstream.WriteLine(""""<body>"""")")
              txtstream.WriteLine("                    $txtstream.WriteLine(""""<script
language='vbscript'>"""")")
              txtstream.WriteLine("    $txtstream.WriteLine("""""") ")
              txtstream.WriteLine("    $txtstream.WriteLine(""""cmd.ActiveConnection
= """""""Provider=" + Provider + ";Data Source=" + fName.Value + ";"""""" """")")
              txtstream.WriteLine("    $txtstream.WriteLine(""""cmd.CommandType =
8"""")")
              txtstream.WriteLine("    $txtstream.WriteLine(""""cmd.CommandText =
""""""""""" + strQuery + """""""""""" """")")
              txtstream.WriteLine("                    $txtstream.WriteLine(""""Call
cmd.Execute()"""")")
              txtstream.WriteLine("    $txtstream.WriteLine("""""") ")
              txtstream.WriteLine("    $txtstream.WriteLine(""""rs.CursorLocation =
3"""")")
              txtstream.WriteLine("    $txtstream.WriteLine(""""rs.LockType = 3"""")")
              txtstream.WriteLine("                    $txtstream.WriteLine(""""Call
rs.Open(cmd)"""")")
              txtstream.WriteLine("    $txtstream.WriteLine("""""") ")
              txtstream.WriteLine("                    $txtstream.WriteLine(Chr(60)    +
""""/script>"""")")


         Case "rs"

              txtstream.WriteLine("                    $txtstream.WriteLine(""""<object
id="""""""rs"""""""                    CLASSID="""""""clsid:00000535-0000-0010-8000-
00AA006D2EA4"""""""" height="""""""0"""""""" width="""""""0""""""""></object>"""")")
              txtstream.WriteLine("    $txtstream.WriteLine(""""</head>"""")")
              txtstream.WriteLine("    $txtstream.WriteLine(""""<body>"""")")
              txtstream.WriteLine("                    $txtstream.WriteLine(""""<script
language='vbscript'>"""")")
              txtstream.WriteLine("    $txtstream.WriteLine("""""") ")
```

```
                txtstream.WriteLine("      $txtstream.WriteLine(""""rs.ActiveConnection =
""""""Provider=" + Provider + ";Data Source=" + fName.Value + ";"""""" "")")
                txtstream.WriteLine("    $txtstream.WriteLine(""""rs.LockType = 3"")")
                txtstream.WriteLine("       $txtstream.WriteLine(""""rs.Cursorlocation =
3"")")
                txtstream.WriteLine("    $txtstream.WriteLine(""""rs.Source = """""""" +
strQuery + """""""" "")")
                txtstream.WriteLine("    $txtstream.WriteLine(""""Call rs.Open"")")
                txtstream.WriteLine("    $txtstream.WriteLine("""") ")
                txtstream.WriteLine("                    $txtstream.WriteLine(Chr(60)     +
""/script>"")")
```

        End Select

        If Orientation = "Multi Line Horizontal" then

        Select Case TableType

            Case "Table"

```
                txtstream.WriteLine("          $txtstream.WriteLine(""""<table  Border='1'
cellpadding='1' cellspacing='1' datasrc=#rs>"")")
```

            Case "Report"

```
                txtstream.WriteLine("          $txtstream.WriteLine(""""<table  Border='0'
cellpadding='1' cellspacing='1' datasrc=#rs>"")")
```

        End Select

        Else

        Select Case TableType

            Case "Table"

```
                txtstream.WriteLine("          $txtstream.WriteLine(""""<table  Border='1'
cellpadding='1' cellspacing='1'>"")")
```

            Case "Report"
```
```

```vbscript
            txtstream.WriteLine("          $txtstream.WriteLine(""""<table  Border='0'
cellpadding='1' cellspacing='1'>"""")")

        End Select


    End If


    else

        txtstream.WriteLine("   $txtstream.WriteLine(""""</head>"""")")
        txtstream.WriteLine("   $txtstream.WriteLine(""""<body>"""")")

    End If

End Sub

Sub Write_The_Happy_Ending()

        txtstream.WriteLine("   $txtstream.WriteLine(""""</table>"""")")
        txtstream.WriteLine("   $txtstream.WriteLine(""""</body>"""")")
        txtstream.WriteLine("   $txtstream.WriteLine(""""</html>"""")")
        txtstream.WriteLine("   $txtstream.Close()")
        txtstream.Close

        tempstr = ""
        Set ws = createObject("WScript.Shell")
        Set fso = CreateObject("Scripting.FileSystemObject")
        Set txtstream = fso.OpenTextFile(ws.CurrentDirectory + "\" + Tablename +
".ps1", 1, true, -2)
        Do While txtstream.AtEndOfStream = false
            tempstr = tempstr + txtstream.ReadLine()
            if Stylesheet = "InLine" then
                tempstr = replace(tempstr, "<th>", "<th style='font-family:Calibri,
Sans-Serif;font-size: 12px;color:darkred;'>")
                tempstr = replace(tempstr, "<td>", "<td style='font-family:Calibri,
Sans-Serif;font-size: 12px;color:navy;'>")
            End If
```

```
                tempstr = tempstr + vbcrlf
        loop
        txtstream.Close
        textarea1.innerText = tempstr

    End Sub


    Sub Do_Static()


        Select Case TableType

            Case "Table"

                txtstream.WriteLine("    $txtstream.WriteLine(""""<table  Border='1'
    cellpadding='1' cellspacing='1'>"""")")

            Case "Report"

                txtstream.WriteLine("    $txtstream.WriteLine(""""<table  Border='0'
    cellpadding='1' cellspacing='1'>"""")")

        End Select

        Select Case Orientation

            Case "Single Line Horizontal"

                txtstream.WriteLine("  $txtstream.WriteLine(""""<tr>"""")")
                txtstream.WriteLine("  for($x=0;$x -lt $rs.Fields.Count;$x++)")
                txtstream.WriteLine("  {")
                txtstream.WriteLine("              $txtstream.WriteLine(""""<th>""""  +
    $rs.Fields.Item($x).Name + """"</th>"""")")
                txtstream.WriteLine("  }")
                txtstream.WriteLine("  $txtstream.WriteLine(""""</tr>"""")")
                txtstream.WriteLine("  $txtstream.WriteLine(""""<tr>"""")")
                txtstream.WriteLine("  for($x=0;$x -lt $rs.Fields.Count;$x++)")
                txtstream.WriteLine("  {")
```

```
        txtstream.WriteLine("                                    [string]$Value    =
$rs.Fields.Item($x).get_Value()")
        txtstream.WriteLine("                         $txtstream.WriteLine(""<td>"    +
Do_Unbound_Controls(""" + $Value + """) + "</td>""")")
        txtstream.WriteLine("    }")
        txtstream.WriteLine("    $txtstream.WriteLine(""</tr>""")")


    Case "Multi-Line Horizontal"

        txtstream.WriteLine("    $txtstream.WriteLine(""<tr>""")")
        txtstream.WriteLine("    for($x=0;$x -lt $rs.Fields.Count;$x++)")
        txtstream.WriteLine("    {")
        txtstream.WriteLine("                      $txtstream.WriteLine(""<th>"""    +
$rs.Fields.Item($x).Name + """</th>""")")
        txtstream.WriteLine("    }")
        txtstream.WriteLine("    $txtstream.WriteLine(""</tr>""")")
        txtstream.WriteLine("    While($rs.EOF -eq $False)")
        txtstream.WriteLine("    {")
        txtstream.WriteLine("        $txtstream.WriteLine(""<tr>""")")
        txtstream.WriteLine("        for($x=0;$x -lt $rs.Fields.Count;$x++)")
        txtstream.WriteLine("        {")
        txtstream.WriteLine("                               [string]$Value    =
$rs.Fields.Item($x).get_Value()")
        txtstream.WriteLine("                          $txtstream.WriteLine(""<td>"    +
Do_Unbound_Controls(""" + $Value + """) + "</td>""")")
        txtstream.WriteLine("        }")
        txtstream.WriteLine("        $txtstream.WriteLine(""</tr>""")")
        txtstream.WriteLine("        $rs.MoveNext()")
        txtstream.WriteLine("    }")


    Case "Single-Line Vertical"

        txtstream.WriteLine("    for($x=0;$x -lt rs.Fields.Count;$x++)")
        txtstream.WriteLine("    {")
        txtstream.WriteLine("                               [string]$Value    =
$rs.Fields.Item($x).get_Value()")
        txtstream.WriteLine("                     $txtstream.WriteLine(""<tr><th>"""    +
$rs.Fields.Item($x).Name + """</th><td>" + Do_Unbound_Controls(""" + $Value +
""") + "</td>""")")
```

```
            txtstream.WriteLine("    }")

        Case "Multi-Line Vertical"

            txtstream.WriteLine("    for($x=0;$x -lt $rs.Fields.Count;$x++)")
            txtstream.WriteLine("    {")
            txtstream.WriteLine("                        $txtstream.WriteLine(""<tr><th>"" +
$rs.Fields.Item($x).Name + ""</th>"")")
            txtstream.WriteLine("        $rs.MoveFirst()")
            txtstream.WriteLine("        While($rs.EOF -eq $false)")
            txtstream.WriteLine("        {")
            txtstream.WriteLine("                                [string]$Value =
$rs.Fields.Item($x).get_Value()")
            txtstream.WriteLine("                        $txtstream.WriteLine(""<td>" +
Do_Unbound_Controls(""" + $Value + """) + "</td>"")")
            txtstream.WriteLine("            $rs.MoveNext()")
            txtstream.WriteLine("        }")
            txtstream.WriteLine("        $txtstream.WriteLine(""</tr>"")")
            txtstream.WriteLine("    }")

    End Select

    End Sub

    Sub Do_Dynamic()


        txtstream.WriteLine("                            $txtstream.WriteLine(""<script
language='vbscript'>"")")


        Select Case TableType

        Case "Table"

            txtstream.WriteLine("
$txtstream.WriteLine(""document.WriteLn(""""""<table  Border='1'  cellpadding='1'
cellspacing='1'>"""")"")")

        Case "Report"
```

```
        txtstream.WriteLine("
$txtstream.WriteLine(""docuemnt.WriteLn(""""""<table   Border='0'  cellpadding='1'
cellspacing='1'>"""""")"""")")

        End Select

    Select Case Orientation

        Case "Single Line Horizontal"

            txtstream.WriteLine("
$txtstream.WriteLine(""document.WriteLn(""""""<tr>"""""")"""")")
            txtstream.WriteLine("   for($x=0;$x -lt $rs.Fields.Count;$x++)")
            txtstream.WriteLine("   {")
            txtstream.WriteLine("
$txtstream.WriteLine(""document.WriteLn(""""""<th>"""" + $rs.Fields.Item($x).Name
+ """"</th>"""""")"""")")
            txtstream.WriteLine("   }")
            txtstream.WriteLine("
$txtstream.WriteLine(""document.WriteLn(""""""</tr>"""""")"""")")
            txtstream.WriteLine("
$txtstream.WriteLine(""document.WriteLn(""""""<tr>"""""")"""")")
            txtstream.WriteLine("   for($x=0;$x -lt $rs.Fields.Count;$x++)")
            txtstream.WriteLine("   {")
            txtstream.WriteLine("                                        [string]$Value    =
$rs.Fields.Item($x).get_Value()")
            txtstream.WriteLine("
$txtstream.WriteLine(""document.WriteLn(""""""<td>"                          +
Do_Unbound_Controls("""" + $Value + """") + "</td>"""""")"""")")
            txtstream.WriteLine("   }")
            txtstream.WriteLine("
$txtstream.WriteLine(""document.WriteLn(""""""</tr>"""""")"""")")


        Case "Multi-Line Horizontal"

            txtstream.WriteLine("
$txtstream.WriteLine(""document.WriteLn(""""""<tr>"""""")"""")")
            txtstream.WriteLine("   for($x=0;$x -lt $rs.Fields.Count;$x++)")
```

```
            txtstream.WriteLine("   {")
            txtstream.WriteLine("
$txtstream.WriteLine(""""document.WriteLn(""""""<th>"""" + $rs.Fields.Item($x).Name
+ """"</th>"""""")"""")""")
            txtstream.WriteLine("   }")
            txtstream.WriteLine("
$txtstream.WriteLine(""""document.WriteLn(""""""</tr>"""""")"""")""")
            txtstream.WriteLine("   while($rs.EOF -eq $False)")
            txtstream.WriteLine("   {")
            txtstream.WriteLine("      $txtstream.WriteLine(""""<tr>"""""")"""")")
            txtstream.WriteLine("      for($x=0;$x -lt $rs.Fields.Count;$x++)")
            txtstream.WriteLine("      {")
            txtstream.WriteLine("                                    [string]$Value   =
$rs.Fields.Item($x).get_Value()")
            txtstream.WriteLine("
$txtstream.WriteLine(""""document.WriteLn(""""""<td>"                         +
Do_Unbound_Controls("""" + $Value + """") + "</td>"""""")"""")""")
            txtstream.WriteLine("      }")
            txtstream.WriteLine("
$txtstream.WriteLine(""""document.WriteLn(""""""</tr>"""""")"""")""")
            txtstream.WriteLine("      $rs.MoveNext()")
            txtstream.WriteLine("   }")

      Case "Single-Line Vertical"

            txtstream.WriteLine("   for($x=0;$x -lt rs.Fields.Count;$x++)")
            txtstream.WriteLine("   {")
            txtstream.WriteLine("                                    [string]$Value    =
$rs.Fields.Item($x).get_Value()")
            txtstream.WriteLine("
$txtstream.WriteLine(""""document.WriteLn(""""""<tr><th>""""                         +
$rs.Fields.Item($x).Name + """"</th><td>" + Do_Unbound_Controls("""" + $Value +
"""") + "</td>"""""")"""")""")
            txtstream.WriteLine("   }")

      Case "Multi-Line Vertical"

            txtstream.WriteLine("   for($x=0;$x -lt $rs.Fields.Count;$x++)")
            txtstream.WriteLine("   {")
```

```
        txtstream.WriteLine("
$txtstream.WriteLine(""document.WriteLn("""""<tr><th>""                    +
$rs.Fields.Item($x).Name + ""</th>"""""")"""")")
        txtstream.WriteLine("     $rs.MoveFirst()")
        txtstream.WriteLine("     while($rs.EOF -eq $False)")
        txtstream.WriteLine("     {")
        txtstream.WriteLine("                              [string]$Value    =
$rs.Fields.Item($x).get_Value()")
        txtstream.WriteLine("
$txtstream.WriteLine(""document.WriteLn("""""<td>"                          +
Do_Unbound_Controls(""""" + $Value + """"") + "</td>"""""")"""")")
        txtstream.WriteLine("        $rs.MoveNext()")
        txtstream.WriteLine("     }")
        txtstream.WriteLine("
$txtstream.WriteLine(""document.WriteLn("""""</tr>"""""")"""")")
        txtstream.WriteLine("   }")

    End Select

    txtstream.WriteLine("
$txtstream.WriteLine(""document.WriteLn("""""</table>"""""")"""")")
    txtstream.WriteLine("   $txtstream.WriteLine(""""" + chr(60) + "/script>"")")

  End Sub

  Sub Do_Cloaked()

    txtstream.WriteLine("                          $txtstream.WriteLine(""<script
language='vbscript'>"")")
    txtstream.WriteLine("  $txtstream.WriteLine(""""")")
    txtstream.WriteLine("  $txtstream.WriteLine(""Dim mystr"")")
    txtstream.WriteLine("  $txtstream.WriteLine(""""")")
    txtstream.WriteLine("  $txtstream.WriteLine(""Sub Window_OnLoad()"")")
    txtstream.WriteLine("  $txtstream.WriteLine(""""")")

    Select Case TableType

      Case "Table"
```

```
        txtstream.WriteLine("          $txtstream.WriteLine(""""mystr = mystr +
""""""<table Border='1' cellpadding='1' cellspacing='1'>"""""" + vbcrlf""")")

    Case "Report"

        txtstream.WriteLine("          $txtstream.WriteLine(""""mystr = mystr +
""""""<table Border='0' cellpadding='1' cellspacing='1'>"""""" + vbcrlf""")")

    End Select

    Select Case Orientation


    Case "Single Line Horizontal"

        txtstream.WriteLine("          $txtstream.WriteLine(""""mystr = mystr &
""""""<tr>"""""" & vbcrlf""")")
        txtstream.WriteLine("  for($x=0;$x -lt $rs.Fields.Count;$x++)")
        txtstream.WriteLine("  {")
        txtstream.WriteLine("          $txtstream.WriteLine(""""mystr = mystr &
""""""<th>"""" + $rs.Fields.Item($x).Name + """"</th>"""""" & vbcrlf""")")
        txtstream.WriteLine("  }")
        txtstream.WriteLine("          $txtstream.WriteLine(""""mystr = mystr &
""""""</tr>"""""" & vbcrlf""")")
        txtstream.WriteLine("          $txtstream.WriteLine(""""mystr = mystr &
""""""<tr>"""""" & vbcrlf""")")
        txtstream.WriteLine("  for($x=0;$x -lt $rs.Fields.Count;$x++)")
        txtstream.WriteLine("  {")
        txtstream.WriteLine("                          [string]$Value =
$rs.Fields.Item($x).get_Value()")
        txtstream.WriteLine("          $txtstream.WriteLine(""""mystr = mystr &
""""""<td>" + Do_Unbound_Controls("""" + $Value + """") + "</td>"""""" &
vbcrlf""")")
        txtstream.WriteLine("  }")
        txtstream.WriteLine("          $txtstream.WriteLine(""""mystr = mystr &
""""""</tr>"""""" & vbcrlf""")")


    Case "Multi-Line Horizontal"
```

```
        txtstream.WriteLine("        $txtstream.WriteLine("""mystr = mystr &
"""""<tr>"""""" & vbcrlf""")")
        txtstream.WriteLine("    for($x=0;$x -lt $rs.Fields.Count;$x++)")
        txtstream.WriteLine("    {")
        txtstream.WriteLine("        $txtstream.WriteLine("""mystr = mystr &
"""""<th>""" + $rs.Fields.Item($x).Name + """</th>"""""" & vbcrlf""")")
        txtstream.WriteLine("    }")
        txtstream.WriteLine("        $txtstream.WriteLine("""mystr = mystr &
"""""</tr>"""""" & vbcrlf""")")
        txtstream.WriteLine("    while($rs.EOF -eq $False)")
        txtstream.WriteLine("    {")
        txtstream.WriteLine("            $txtstream.WriteLine("""<tr>"""""" &
vbcrlf""")")
        txtstream.WriteLine("      for($x=0;$x -lt $rs.Fields.Count;$x++)")
        txtstream.WriteLine("      {")
        txtstream.WriteLine("                    [string]$Value =
$rs.Fields.Item($x).get_Value()")
        txtstream.WriteLine("            $txtstream.WriteLine("""mystr = mystr &
"""""<td>" + Do_Unbound_Controls("""" + $Value + """") + "</td>"""""" &
vbcrlf""")")
        txtstream.WriteLine("      }")
        txtstream.WriteLine("            $txtstream.WriteLine("""mystr = mystr &
"""""</tr>"""""" & vbcrlf""")")
        txtstream.WriteLine("      $rs.MoveNext()")
        txtstream.WriteLine("    }")

    Case "Single-Line Vertical"

        txtstream.WriteLine("    for($x=0;$x -lt rs.Fields.Count;$x++)")
        txtstream.WriteLine("    {")
        txtstream.WriteLine("                        [string]$Value =
$rs.Fields.Item($x).get_Value()")
        txtstream.WriteLine("            $txtstream.WriteLine("""mystr = mystr &
"""""<tr><th>"""    +    $rs.Fields.Item($x).Name    +    """</th><td>"    +
Do_Unbound_Controls("""" + $Value + """") + "</td>"""""" & vbcrlf""")")
        txtstream.WriteLine("    }")

    Case "Multi-Line Vertical"

        txtstream.WriteLine("    For($x=0;$x -lt $rs.Fields.Count;$x++)")
```

```
            txtstream.WriteLine("    {")
            txtstream.WriteLine("                $txtstream.WriteLine(""mystr = mystr &
""""""<tr><th>"" + $rs.Fields.Item($x).Name + ""</th>"""""" & vbcrlf"")")
            txtstream.WriteLine("        $rs.MoveFirst()")
            txtstream.WriteLine("        while($rs.EOF -eq $False)")
            txtstream.WriteLine("        {")
            txtstream.WriteLine("                                [string]$Value =
$rs.Fields.Item($x).get_Value()")
            txtstream.WriteLine("                $txtstream.WriteLine(""mystr = mystr &
""""""<td>"" + Do_Unbound_Controls("""" + $Value + """") + ""</td>"""""" &
vbcrlf"")")
            txtstream.WriteLine("            $rs.MoveNext()")
            txtstream.WriteLine("        }")
            txtstream.WriteLine("                $txtstream.WriteLine(""mystr = mystr &
""""""</tr>"""""" & vbcrlf"")")
            txtstream.WriteLine("    }")

        End Select

        txtstream.WriteLine("    $txtstream.WriteLine("""""")")
        txtstream.WriteLine("            $txtstream.WriteLine(""mystr    =    mystr    &
""""""</table>"""""" & vbcrlf"")")
        txtstream.WriteLine("    $txtstream.WriteLine("""""")")
        txtstream.WriteLine("
$txtstream.WriteLine(""document.WriteLn(mystr)"")")
        txtstream.WriteLine("    $txtstream.WriteLine("""""")")
        txtstream.WriteLine("    $txtstream.WriteLine(""End Sub"")")
        txtstream.WriteLine("    $txtstream.WriteLine("""""")")
        txtstream.WriteLine("    $txtstream.WriteLine("""" + chr(60) + "/script>"")")

    End Sub

    Sub Do_Bound()


        Select Case Orientation


            Case "Single-Line Horizontal"
```

```
            txtstream.WriteLine("   $txtstream.WriteLine(""<tr>"")")
            txtstream.WriteLine("   for($x=0;$x -lt $rs.Fields.Count;$x++)")
            txtstream.WriteLine("   {")
            txtstream.WriteLine("                    $txtstream.WriteLine(""<th>""   +
$rs.Fields.Item($x).Name + ""</th>"")")
            txtstream.WriteLine("   }")
            txtstream.WriteLine("   $txtstream.WriteLine(""</tr>"")")
            txtstream.WriteLine("   $txtstream.WriteLine(""<tr>"")")
            txtstream.WriteLine("   for($x=0;$x -lt $rs.Fields.Count;$x++)")
            txtstream.WriteLine("   {")
            txtstream.WriteLine("                    $txtstream.WriteLine(""<td>"   +
do_Bound_Controls("Single", """ + $rs.Fields.Item($x).Name + """) + "</td>"")")
            txtstream.WriteLine("   }")
            txtstream.WriteLine("   $txtstream.WriteLine(""</tr>"")")


        Case "Multi-Line Horizontal"


            txtstream.WriteLine("   $txtstream.WriteLine(""<tr>"")")
            txtstream.WriteLine("   for($x=0;$x -lt $rs.Fields.Count;$x++)")
            txtstream.WriteLine("   {")
            txtstream.WriteLine("                    $txtstream.WriteLine(""<th>""   +
$rs.Fields.Item($x).Name + ""</th>"")")
            txtstream.WriteLine("   }")
            txtstream.WriteLine("   $txtstream.WriteLine(""</tr>"")")
            txtstream.WriteLine("   $txtstream.WriteLine(""<tr>"")")
            txtstream.WriteLine("   for($x=0;$x  lt $rs.Fields.Count;$x++)")
            txtstream.WriteLine("   {")
            txtstream.WriteLine("                    $txtstream.WriteLine(""<td>"   +
do_Bound_Controls("Multi", """ + $rs.Fields.Item($x).Name + """) + "</td>"")")
            txtstream.WriteLine("   }")
            txtstream.WriteLine("   $txtstream.WriteLine(""</tr>"")")


        Case "Single-Line Vertical"

            txtstream.WriteLine("   for($x=0;$x -lt $rs.Fields.Count;$x++)")
            txtstream.WriteLine("   {")
```

```
            txtstream.WriteLine("                    $txtstream.WriteLine(""<tr><th>"" +
$rs.Fields.Item($x).Name + ""</th><td>" + do_Bound_Controls("Single", """" +
$rs.Fields.Item($x).Name + """") + "</td></tr>"")")
            txtstream.WriteLine("   }")

    End Select

  End Sub


  Function Do_Unbound_Controls(ByVal Value)

      Dim mystr

      Select Case ControlType

        Case "None"

          mystr = Value

        Case "Button"

          mystr = "<button value='" + Value + "' style='Width:100%'></button>"

        Case "Checkbox"

          mystr  =  "<label><input  type='checkbox'  value='"  +  Value  +
"'></input>" + Value + "</label>"

        Case "Combobox"

          mystr = mystr + "<select style='width:100%;'><option Value='" + Value
+ "'>" + Value + "</option></select>"

        Case "Div"

          mystr = "<div>" + Value + "</div>"
```

```
        Case "Input Button"

                mystr   =   "<input    type='button'   value='"   +   Value   +   "'
style='Width:100%'></input>"

        Case "Label"

            mystr = "<Label>" + Value + "<Label>"

        Case "Listbox"

                mystr   =   "<select   multiple=""""true""""   style='width:100%;'><option
Value='" + Value + "'>" + Value + "</option></select>"

        Case "Radio Button"

            mystr = "<input type='radio' Value='" + Value + "'></input>"

        Case "Span"

            mystr = "<span>" + Value + "</span>"

        Case "Textbox"

            mystr = "<input type='text' Value='" + Value + "'></input>"

        Case "Textarea"

            mystr = "<textarea>" + Value + "</textarea>"

    End Select

    Do_Unbound_Controls = mystr

End Function


Function Do_Bound_Controls(ByVal BindingType, ByVal Value)
```

```vb
If BindingType = "Single" Then

    Dim mystr

    Select Case ControlType

        Case "None"

            mystr = "<span datasrc=#rs datafld='" + Value + "'></span>"

        Case "Button"

            mystr = "<input type='button' datasrc=#rs datafld='" + Value + "' style='Width:100%'></input>"

        Case "Checkbox"

            mystr = "<label><input type='checkbox' datasrc=#rs datafld='" + Value + "'></input><label datasrc=#rs datafld='" + Value + "'></label>"

        Case "Div"

            mystr = "<div datasrc=#rs datafld='" + Value + "'></div>"

        Case "Label"

            mystr = "<label datasrc=#rs datafld='" + Value + "'></label>"

        Case "Radio Button"

            mystr = "<input type='radio' datasrc=#rs datafld='" + Value + "'></input><label datasrc=#rs datafld='" + Value + "'></label>"

        Case "Span"

            mystr = "<span datasrc=#rs datafld='" + Value + "'></span>"
```

Case "Textbox"

mystr = "<input type='text' datasrc=#rs datafld='" + Value + "'></input>"

Case "Textarea"

mystr = "<textarea datasrc=#rs datafld='" + Value + "'></textarea>"

End Select

Do_Bound_Controls mystr

Else

Select Case ControlType

Case "None"

mystr = "<span datafld='" + Value + "'></span>"

Case "Button"

mystr = "<input type='button' datafld='" + Value + "' style='Width:100%'></input>"

Case "Checkbox"

mystr = "<label><input type='checkbox' datafld='" + Value + "'></input><label datasrc=#rs datafld='" + Value + "'></label>"

Case "Div"

mystr = "<div datafld='" + Value + "'></div>"

Case "Label"

mystr = "<label datafld='" + Value + "'></label>"

```vb
        Case "Radio Button"

            mystr = "<input type='radio' datafld='" + Value + "'></input><label
datasrc=#rs datafld='" + Value + "'></label>"

        Case "Span"

            mystr = "<span datafld='" + Value + "'></span>"

        Case "Textbox"

            mystr = "<input type='text' datafld='" + Value + "'></input>"

        Case "Textarea"

            mystr = "<textarea datafld='" + Value + "'></textarea>"

    End Select

    Do_Bound_Controls = mystr

End If


End Function


Sub LT1_OnClick()

    If fName.Value = "" then
        msgbox("Please provide the location and name of the database you want to
use before clicking here.")
        exit sub
    else
        cnstr = "Provider=" + Provider + ";Data Source = " + FName.Value + ";"

        Set cn = CreateObject("ADODB.Connection")
        On Error Resume Next
        cn.ConnectionString = cnstr
```

```
        Call cn.Open
        if err.number = 0 then
            Set ws = CreateObject("WScript.Shell")
            Set fso = CreateObject("Scripting.FileSystemObject")
            Set txtstream = fso.OpenTextFile(ws.CurrentDirectory + "\tables.txt", 2,
true, -2)
            Set rs1 = cn.OpenSchema(20)
            Dim l()
            Redim l(3)
            l(0) = Len("Tablename")
            l(1) = Len("TableType")
            l(2) = Len("Description")

            Do While rs1.EOF = false
                if len(rs1.Fields("TABLE_NAME").Value) > l(0) then
                    l(0) = len(rs1.Fields("TABLE_NAME").Value)
                End If

                if len(rs1.Fields("TABLE_TYPE").Value) > l(1) then
                    l(1) = len(rs1.Fields("TABLE_TYPE").Value)
                End If

                if len(rs1.Fields("TABLE_DESCRIPTION").Value) > l(2) then
                    l(2) = len(rs1.Fields("TABLE_DESCRIPTION").Value)
                End If

                rs1.MoveNext
            Loop

            rs1.MoveFirst

            l(0) = l(0) + 3
            l(1) = l(1) + 3
            l(2) = l(2) + 3

            Dim v

            v = l(0) - Len("Tablename")
            mystr = "Tablename" + space(v)
            v = l(1) - Len("TableType")
```

```
mystr = mystr + "TableType" + space(v)
v = l(2) - Len("Description")
mystr = mystr + "Description" + space(v)
txtstream.WriteLine(mystr)
mystr = ""
txtstream.WriteLine("")

Set tbl = document.GetElementByID("trex")
tbl.innerHTML = ""
Set opt = document.createElement("option")
opt.value = "*Select An Option*"
opt.text = "*Select An Option*"
opt.Selected = true
tbl.Options.Add(opt)




Do While rs1.EOF = false



  If mid(rs1.Fields("TABLE_NAME").Value, 1,4) <> "MSys" then

    If rs1.Fields("TABLE_TYPE").Value = "TABLE" then
      Set opt = document.createElement("option")
      opt.value = rs1.Fields("TABLE_NAME").Value
      opt.text = rs1.Fields("TABLE_NAME").Value
      tbl.Options.Add(opt)
    End If

        v = l(0) - Len(rs1.Fields("TABLE_NAME").Value)
        mystr = rs1.Fields("TABLE_NAME").Value + space(v)
        v = l(1) - Len(rs1.Fields("TABLE_TYPE").Value)
        mystr = mystr + rs1.Fields("TABLE_TYPE").Value + space(v)
        v = l(2) - Len(rs1.Fields("DESCRIPTION").Value)
        mystr = mystr + rs1.Fields("DESCRIPTION").Value
        txtstream.WriteLine(mystr)
        mystr = ""
  End If
  rs1.MoveNext
```

```
            Loop

            Dim tempstr
            tempstr = ""
            Set txtstream = fso.OpenTextFile(ws.CurrentDirectory + "\tables.txt", 1,
true, -2)
            Do While txtstream.AtEndOfStream = false
               tempstr = tempstr + txtstream.ReadLine()
               tempstr = tempstr + vbcrlf
            loop
            txtstream.Close
            textarea1.innerText = tempstr
         Else

            msgbox("Test connection Failed with: " + err.Description)

         End IF

      End If

      strQuery = ""

   End Sub

   Sub TestConnection1_OnClick()

      If fName.Value = "" then
            msgbox("Please provide the location and name of the database you want to
use before clicking here.")
            exit sub
      else
         cnstr = "Provider=" + Provider + ";Data Source = " + FName.Value + ";"
         Set cn = CreateObject("ADODB.Connection")
         On Error Resume Next
         cn.ConnectionString = cnstr
         Call cn.Open
         if err.number = 0 then
            msgbox("Test connection succeeded.")
         else
            msgbox("Connecion failed with: " + err.Description)
```

```vbscript
            End If
         End If

      End Sub

      Sub Search_OnClick()

         Set ws = CreateObject("WScript.Shell")
         Set OpenDialog1 = CreateObject("MSComDlg.CommonDialog")

         With OpenDialog1
            .DialogTitle = "Open Database"
            .InitDir = ws.CurrentDirectory
            .Filter = "Microsoft Older Access Database(*.mdb)|*.mdb|Microsoft Newer
Access Database(*.accdb)|*.accdb"
            .FilterIndex = 2
            .MaxFileSize =32000
            .Flags = 2621952
            .ShowOpen
         End With
         If OpenDialog1.Filename <> "" then
            FName.Value = OpenDialog1.Filename
         End If

      End Sub

      Sub DataLinks1_OnClick()

      Set cn = createObject("ADODB.Connection")
      Set dl = CreateObject("Datalinks")
      Set cn = dl.PromptNew()
      Provider= cn.Provider
      cnstr = cn.ConnectionString
      FName.Value = cn.Properties("Data Source").Value

      End Sub

      Sub Clipboard1_OnClick()

         Set range = Textarea1.createTextRange()
```

```vbscript
    call range.findText(Textarea1.InnerText)
    range.select
    Call document.execCommand("Copy")
    Call document.execCommand("Unselect")

End Sub


Sub Providers_OnClick()

    Const HKEY_LOCAL_MACHINE = &H80000002
    strComputer = "."
    Dim strValue
    Set                         oReg                         =
GetObject("winmgmts:{impersonationLevel=impersonate}!\\.\root\default:StdRegPr
ov")
    oReg.EnumKey                         HKEY_LOCAL_MACHINE,
"SOFTWARE\Wow6432Node\Classes\CLSID", SubKeyNames
    mystr           =           "Providers       found       in
HKEY_LOCAL_MACHINE\SOFTWARE\Wow6432Node\Classes\CLSID" + vbCrLf
    For Each skn In SubKeyNames
        If                      oReg.GetStringValue(HKEY_LOCAL_MACHINE,
"SOFTWARE\Wow6432Node\Classes\CLSID\" + skn + "\Ole Db Provider", "",
strValue) = 0 Then
            oReg.GetStringValue                  HKEY_LOCAL_MACHINE,
"SOFTWARE\Wow6432Node\Classes\CLSID\" + skn, "", strValue
        mystr = mystr + strValue + vbCrLf
        End If
    Next
    mystr = mystr + "" + vbCrLf
    Textarea1.innerText = mystr

End Sub

Sub Drivers_OnClick()

    const HKEY_LOCAL_MACHINE = &H80000002
    strComputer = "."
```

```vbscript
    Set                                                                 oReg=
GetObject("winmgmts:{impersonationLevel=impersonate}!\\.\root\default:StdRegPr
ov")


    if              oReg.EnumValues              (HKEY_LOCAL_MACHINE,
"SOFTWARE\Wow6432Node\ODBC\ODBCINST.INI\ODBC  Drivers", SubKeyNames) =
0 Then
        mystr         =         "Drivers         found         in
HKEY_LOCAL_MACHINE\SOFTWARE\Wow6432Node\ODBC\ODBCINST.INI\ODBC
Drivers" + vbcrlf
        mystr = mystr + "" + vbcrlf
        for each skn in SubKeyNames
            mystr = mystr + skn + vbcrlf
        Next
        mystr = mystr + "" + vbcrlf
        Textarea1.innerText = mystr
    End If

End Sub

Sub ISAMS_OnClick()

Dim tempstr
Dim SubKeyNames

const HKEY_LOCAL_MACHINE = &H80000002
strComputer = "."
    Set                                                                 oreg=
GetObject("winmgmts:{impersonationLevel=impersonate}!\\.\root\default:StdRegPr
ov")
    if                              oreg.EnumKey(HKEY_LOCAL_MACHINE,
"SOFTWARE\Wow6432Node\Microsoft\Jet 3.5\ISAM Formats", SubKeyNames) = 0
then
        mystr        =        "Found     Jet     3.5     ISAMS     in
HKEY_LOCAL_MACHINE\Wow6432Node\Microsoft\Jet 3.5\ISAM Formats" + vbcrlf
        mystr = mystr + "" + vbcrlf
        for each skn in SubKeyNames
            mystr = mystr + skn + vbcrlf
        Next
        mystr = mystr + "" + vbcrlf
```

```vba
      End If

      if                                oreg.EnumKey(HKEY_LOCAL_MACHINE,
"SOFTWARE\Wow6432Node\Microsoft\Jet 4.0\ISAM Formats", SubKeyNames) = 0
then
          mystr   =   mystr   +   "Found   Jet   4.0   ISAMS   in
HKEY_LOCAL_MACHINE\Wow6432Node\Microsoft\Jet 4.0\ISAM Formats" + vbcrlf
          mystr = mystr + "" + vbcrlf
          for each skn in SubKeyNames
             mystr = mystr + skn + vbcrlf
          Next
          mystr = mystr + "" + vbcrlf
      End If

      if                                oReg.EnumKey(HKEY_LOCAL_MACHINE,
"SOFTWARE\Wow6432Node\Microsoft\Office\10.0\Access Connectivity Engine\ISAM
Formats", SubKeyNames) = 0 then
          mystr   =   mystr   +   "Found   ACE   10.0   ISAMS   in
SOFTWARE\Wow6432Node\Microsoft\Office\10.0\Access  Connectivity  Engine\ISAM
Formats" + vbcrlf
          mystr = mystr + "" + vbcrlf
          for each skn in SubKeyNames
             mystr = mystr + skn + vbcrlf
          Next
          mystr = mystr + "" + vbcrlf
      End If

      if                                oReg.EnumKey(HKEY_LOCAL_MACHINE,
"SOFTWARE\Wow6432Node\Microsoft\Office\12.0\Access  Connectivity  Engine\ISAM
Formats", SubKeyNames) = 0 then
          mystr   =   mystr   +   "Found   ACE   12.0   ISAMS   in
KEY_LOCAL_MACHHINE\SOFTWARE\Wow6432Node\Microsoft\Office\12.0\Access
Connectivity Engine\ISAM Formats" + vbcrlf
          mystr = mystr + "" + vbcrlf
          for each skn in SubKeyNames
             mystr = mystr + skn + vbcrlf
          Next
          mystr = mystr + "" + vbcrlf
      End If
```

```
    if                          oReg.EnumKey(HKEY_LOCAL_MACHINE,
"SOFTWARE\Wow6432Node\Microsoft\Office\14.0\Access Connectivity Engine\ISAM
Formats", SubKeyNames) = 0 then
    mystr    =    mystr    +    "Found    ACE    14.0    ISAMS    in
KEY_LOCAL_MACHHINE\SOFTWARE\Wow6432Node\Microsoft\Office\14.0\Access
Connectivity Engine\ISAM Formats" + vbcrlf
        mystr = mystr + "" + vbcrlf
        for each skn in SubKeyNames
            mystr = mystr + skn + vbcrlf
        Next
        mystr = mystr + "" + vbcrlf
    End If


    if                          oReg.EnumKey(HKEY_LOCAL_MACHINE,
"SOFTWARE\Wow6432Node\Microsoft\Office\15.0\Access Connectivity Engine\ISAM
Formats", SubKeyNames) = 0 then
    mystr    =    mystr    +    "Found    ACE    15.0    ISAMS    in
KEY_LOCAL_MACHHINE\SOFTWARE\Wow6432Node\Microsoft\Office\15.0\Access
Connectivity Engine\ISAM Formats" + vbcrlf
        mystr = mystr + "" + vbcrlf
        for each skn in SubKeyNames
            mystr = mystr + skn + vbcrlf
        Next
        mystr = mystr + "" + vbcrlf
    End If


    if                          oReg.EnumKey(HKEY_LOCAL_MACHINE,
"SOFTWARE\Wow6432Node\Microsoft\Office\16.0\Access Connectivity Engine\ISAM
Formats", SubKeyNames) = 0 then
    mystr    =    mystr    +    "Found    ACE    16.0    ISAMS    in
KEY_LOCAL_MACHHINE\SOFTWARE\Wow6432Node\Microsoft\Office\16.0\Access
Connectivity Engine\ISAM Formats" + vbcrlf
        mystr = mystr + "" + vbcrlf
        for each skn in SubKeyNames
            mystr = mystr + skn + vbcrlf
        Next
        mystr = mystr + "" + vbcrlf
    End If
```

```
Textarea1.innerText = mystr

End Sub

Sub Create_Template()

End Sub

Sub Add_The_StyleSheet()

    Select Case StyleSheet

        Case "None"

        Case "Basic"

            txtstream.WriteLine("                        $txtstream.WriteLine(""""<style
type='text/css'>"""")")
            txtstream.WriteLine("    $txtstream.WriteLine(""""th"""")")
            txtstream.WriteLine("    $txtstream.WriteLine(""""{"""")")
            txtstream.WriteLine("            $txtstream.WriteLine(""""        COLOR:
Darkred;"""")")
            txtstream.WriteLine("    $txtstream.WriteLine(""""}"""")")
            txtstream.WriteLine("    $txtstream.WriteLine(""""td"""")")
            txtstream.WriteLine("    $txtstream.WriteLine(""""{"""")")
            txtstream.WriteLine("    $txtstream.WriteLine(""""    COLOR: navy;"""")")
            txtstream.WriteLine("    $txtstream.WriteLine(""""}"""")")
            txtstream.WriteLine("    $txtstream.WriteLine(""""</style>"""")")

        Case "InLine"


        Case "Table"

            txtstream.WriteLine("                        $txtstream.WriteLine(""""<style
type=text/css>"""")")
            txtstream.WriteLine("    $txtstream.WriteLine(""""#itsthetable {"""")")
            txtstream.WriteLine("    $txtstream.WriteLine("""" font-family:  Georgia,
""""""Times New Roman"""""", Times, serif;"""")")
```

```
txtstream.WriteLine("   $txtstream.WriteLine("""color: #036;""")")
txtstream.WriteLine("   $txtstream.WriteLine("""}""")")

txtstream.WriteLine("   $txtstream.WriteLine("""caption {""")")
txtstream.WriteLine("   $txtstream.WriteLine("""font-size: 48px;""")")
txtstream.WriteLine("   $txtstream.WriteLine("""color: #036;""")")
txtstream.WriteLine("   $txtstream.WriteLine("""font-weight:
bolder;""")")
txtstream.WriteLine("   $txtstream.WriteLine("""font-variant:   small-
caps;""")")
txtstream.WriteLine("   $txtstream.WriteLine("""}""")")

txtstream.WriteLine("   $txtstream.WriteLine("""th {""")")
txtstream.WriteLine("   $txtstream.WriteLine("""font-size: 12px;""")")
txtstream.WriteLine("   $txtstream.WriteLine("""color: #FFF;""")")
txtstream.WriteLine("   $txtstream.WriteLine("""background-color:
#06C;""")")
txtstream.WriteLine("   $txtstream.WriteLine("""padding:          8px
4px;""")")
txtstream.WriteLine("   $txtstream.WriteLine("""border-bottom:   1px
solid #015ebc;""")")
txtstream.WriteLine("   $txtstream.WriteLine("""}""")")

txtstream.WriteLine("   $txtstream.WriteLine("""table {""")")
txtstream.WriteLine("   $txtstream.WriteLine("""margin: 0;""")")
txtstream.WriteLine("   $txtstream.WriteLine("""padding: 0;""")")
txtstream.WriteLine("   $txtstream.WriteLine("""border-collapse:
collapse;""")")
txtstream.WriteLine("   $txtstream.WriteLine("""border:   1px   solid
#06C;""")")
txtstream.WriteLine("   $txtstream.WriteLine("""width: 100%""")")
txtstream.WriteLine("   $txtstream.WriteLine("""}""")")

txtstream.WriteLine("   $txtstream.WriteLine("""#itsthetable th a:link,
#itsthetable th a:visited {""")")
txtstream.WriteLine("   $txtstream.WriteLine("""color: #FFF;""")")
txtstream.WriteLine("   $txtstream.WriteLine("""text-decoration:
none;""")")
txtstream.WriteLine("   $txtstream.WriteLine("""border-left: 5px solid
#FFF;""")")
```

```
txtstream.WriteLine("                    $txtstream.WriteLine("" padding-left:
3px;"")")
txtstream.WriteLine("                    $txtstream.WriteLine(""}"")")

txtstream.WriteLine("                            $txtstream.WriteLine(""th    a:hover,
#itsthetable th a:active {"")")
txtstream.WriteLine("                    $txtstream.WriteLine("" color: #F90;"")")
txtstream.WriteLine("                    $txtstream.WriteLine("" text-decoration: line-
through;"")")
txtstream.WriteLine("                    $txtstream.WriteLine("" border-left: 5px solid
#F90;"")")
txtstream.WriteLine("                    $txtstream.WriteLine("" padding-left:
3px;"")")
txtstream.WriteLine("                    $txtstream.WriteLine(""}"")")

txtstream.WriteLine("                    $txtstream.WriteLine(""tbody th:hover {"")")
txtstream.WriteLine("                    $txtstream.WriteLine("" background-image:
url(imgs/tbody_hover.gif);"")")
txtstream.WriteLine("                    $txtstream.WriteLine("" background-position:
bottom;"")")
txtstream.WriteLine("                    $txtstream.WriteLine("" background-repeat:
repeat-x;"")")
txtstream.WriteLine("                    $txtstream.WriteLine(""}"")")

txtstream.WriteLine("                    $txtstream.WriteLine(""td {"")")
txtstream.WriteLine("                    $txtstream.WriteLine("" background-color:
#f2f2f2;"")")
txtstream.WriteLine("                    $txtstream.WriteLine("" padding: 4px;"")")
txtstream.WriteLine("                    $txtstream.WriteLine("" font-size: 12px;"")")
txtstream.WriteLine("                    $txtstream.WriteLine(""}"")")

txtstream.WriteLine("                    $txtstream.WriteLine(""#itsthetable td:hover
{"")")
txtstream.WriteLine("                    $txtstream.WriteLine("" background-color:
#f8f8f8;"")")

txtstream.WriteLine("                    $txtstream.WriteLine(""}"")")

txtstream.WriteLine("                    $txtstream.WriteLine(""#itsthetable td a:link,
#itsthetable td a:visited {"")")
```

```
txtstream.WriteLine("      $txtstream.WriteLine("""color: #039;""")")
txtstream.WriteLine("      $txtstream.WriteLine("""text-decoration:
none;""")")

txtstream.WriteLine("      $txtstream.WriteLine("""border-left: 3px solid
#039;""")")
txtstream.WriteLine("      $txtstream.WriteLine("""padding-left:
3px;""")")

txtstream.WriteLine("      $txtstream.WriteLine("""}""")")


txtstream.WriteLine("              $txtstream.WriteLine("""#itsthetable   td
a:hover, #itsthetable td a:active {""")")
txtstream.WriteLine("      $txtstream.WriteLine("""color: #06C;""")")
txtstream.WriteLine("      $txtstream.WriteLine("""text-decoration: line-
through;""")")
txtstream.WriteLine("      $txtstream.WriteLine("""border-left: 3px solid
#06C;""")")
txtstream.WriteLine("      $txtstream.WriteLine("""padding-left:
3px;""")")

txtstream.WriteLine("      $txtstream.WriteLine("""}""")")


txtstream.WriteLine("      $txtstream.WriteLine("""#itsthetable th {""")")
txtstream.WriteLine("      $txtstream.WriteLine("""text-align: left;""")")
txtstream.WriteLine("      $txtstream.WriteLine("""width: 150px;""")")
txtstream.WriteLine("      $txtstream.WriteLine("""}""")")


txtstream.WriteLine("      $txtstream.WriteLine("""#itsthetable tr {""")")
txtstream.WriteLine("      $txtstream.WriteLine("""border-bottom:   1px
solid #CCC;""")")
txtstream.WriteLine("      $txtstream.WriteLine("""}""")")


txtstream.WriteLine("      $txtstream.WriteLine("""#itsthetable thead th
{""")")
txtstream.WriteLine("      $txtstream.WriteLine("""background-image:
url(imgs/thead_back.gif);""")")
txtstream.WriteLine("      $txtstream.WriteLine("""background-repeat:
repeat-x;""")")
txtstream.WriteLine("      $txtstream.WriteLine("""background-color:
#06C;""")")
txtstream.WriteLine("      $txtstream.WriteLine("""height: 30px;""")")
txtstream.WriteLine("      $txtstream.WriteLine("""font-size: 18px;""")")
```

```
            txtstream.WriteLine("   $txtstream.WriteLine("" text-align:
center;"")")
            txtstream.WriteLine("   $txtstream.WriteLine("" text-shadow:     #333
2px 2px;"")")
            txtstream.WriteLine("   $txtstream.WriteLine("" border: 2px;"")")
            txtstream.WriteLine("   $txtstream.WriteLine(""}"")")

            txtstream.WriteLine("   $txtstream.WriteLine(""#itsthetable tfoot th
{"")")
            txtstream.WriteLine("   $txtstream.WriteLine("" background-image:
url(imgs/tfoot_back.gif);"")")
            txtstream.WriteLine("   $txtstream.WriteLine("" background-repeat:
repeat-x;"")")
            txtstream.WriteLine("   $txtstream.WriteLine("" background-color:
#036;"")")
            txtstream.WriteLine("   $txtstream.WriteLine("" height: 30px;"")")
            txtstream.WriteLine("   $txtstream.WriteLine("" font-size: 28px;"")")
            txtstream.WriteLine("   $txtstream.WriteLine("" text-align:
center;"")")
            txtstream.WriteLine("   $txtstream.WriteLine("" text-shadow:     #333
2px 2px;"")")
            txtstream.WriteLine("   $txtstream.WriteLine(""}"")")

            txtstream.WriteLine("   $txtstream.WriteLine(""#itsthetable tfoot td
{"")")
            txtstream.WriteLine("   $txtstream.WriteLine("" background-image:
url(imgs/tfoot_back.gif);"")")
            txtstream.WriteLine("   $txtstream.WriteLine("" background-repeat:
repeat-x;"")")
            txtstream.WriteLine("   $txtstream.WriteLine("" background-color:
#036;"")")
            txtstream.WriteLine("   $txtstream.WriteLine("" color: FFF;"")")
            txtstream.WriteLine("   $txtstream.WriteLine("" height: 30px;"")")
            txtstream.WriteLine("   $txtstream.WriteLine("" font-size: 24px;"")")
            txtstream.WriteLine("   $txtstream.WriteLine("" text-align: left;"")")
            txtstream.WriteLine("   $txtstream.WriteLine("" text-shadow:     #333
2px 2px;"")")
            txtstream.WriteLine("   $txtstream.WriteLine(""}"")")
```

```
                txtstream.WriteLine("              $txtstream.WriteLine(""tbody     td
a[href="""""http://www.csslab.cl/"""""] {""")")
                txtstream.WriteLine("    $txtstream.WriteLine("" font-weight:
bolder;""")")
                txtstream.WriteLine("    $txtstream.WriteLine(""}""")")
                txtstream.WriteLine("    $txtstream.WriteLine(""</style>""")")


        Case "BlackAndWhiteText"


                txtstream.WriteLine("                  $txtstream.WriteLine(""<style
type='text/css'>""")")
                txtstream.WriteLine("    $txtstream.WriteLine(""th""")")
                txtstream.WriteLine("    $txtstream.WriteLine(""{""")")
                txtstream.WriteLine("    $txtstream.WriteLine(""   COLOR: white;""")")
                txtstream.WriteLine("     $txtstream.WriteLine(""     BACKGROUND-
COLOR: black;""")")
                txtstream.WriteLine("          $txtstream.WriteLine(""          FONT-
FAMILY:font-family: Cambria, serif;""")")
                txtstream.WriteLine("        $txtstream.WriteLine(""        FONT-SIZE:
12px;""")")
                txtstream.WriteLine("        $txtstream.WriteLine(""        text-align:
left;""")")
                txtstream.WriteLine("        $txtstream.WriteLine(""        white-Space:
nowrap;""")")
                txtstream.WriteLine("    $txtstream.WriteLine(""}""")")
                txtstream.WriteLine("    $txtstream.WriteLine(""td""")")
                txtstream.WriteLine("    $txtstream.WriteLine(""{""")")
                txtstream.WriteLine("    $txtstream.WriteLine(""   COLOR: white;""")")
                txtstream.WriteLine("     $txtstream.WriteLine(""     BACKGROUND-
COLOR: black;""")")
                txtstream.WriteLine("     $txtstream.WriteLine(""     FONT-FAMILY:
font-family: Cambria, serif;""")")
                txtstream.WriteLine("        $txtstream.WriteLine(""        FONT-SIZE:
12px;""")")
                txtstream.WriteLine("        $txtstream.WriteLine(""        text-align:
left;""")")
                txtstream.WriteLine("        $txtstream.WriteLine(""        white-Space:
nowrap;""")")
```

```
txtstream.WriteLine("    $txtstream.WriteLine(""}""')")
txtstream.WriteLine("    $txtstream.WriteLine(""div""')")
txtstream.WriteLine("    $txtstream.WriteLine(""{""')")
txtstream.WriteLine("    $txtstream.WriteLine(""    COLOR: white;""')")
txtstream.WriteLine("    $txtstream.WriteLine(""    BACKGROUND-
COLOR: black;""')")
txtstream.WriteLine("    $txtstream.WriteLine(""    FONT-FAMILY:
font-family: Cambria, serif;""')")
txtstream.WriteLine("    $txtstream.WriteLine(""    FONT-SIZE:
10px;""')")
txtstream.WriteLine("    $txtstream.WriteLine(""    text-align:
left;""')")
txtstream.WriteLine("    $txtstream.WriteLine(""    white-Space:
nowrap;""')")
txtstream.WriteLine("    $txtstream.WriteLine(""}""')")
txtstream.WriteLine("    $txtstream.WriteLine(""span""')")
txtstream.WriteLine("    $txtstream.WriteLine(""{""')")
txtstream.WriteLine("    $txtstream.WriteLine(""    COLOR: white;""')")
txtstream.WriteLine("    $txtstream.WriteLine(""    BACKGROUND-
COLOR: black;""')")
txtstream.WriteLine("    $txtstream.WriteLine(""    FONT-FAMILY:
font-family: Cambria, serif;""')")
txtstream.WriteLine("    $txtstream.WriteLine(""    FONT-SIZE:
10px;""')")
txtstream.WriteLine("    $txtstream.WriteLine(""    text-align:
left;""')")
txtstream.WriteLine("    $txtstream.WriteLine(""    white-Space:
nowrap;""')")
txtstream.WriteLine("    $txtstream.WriteLine(""    display:inline-
block;""')")
txtstream.WriteLine("    $txtstream.WriteLine(""    width: 100%;""')")
txtstream.WriteLine("    $txtstream.WriteLine(""}""')")
txtstream.WriteLine("    $txtstream.WriteLine(""textarea""')")
txtstream.WriteLine("    $txtstream.WriteLine(""{""')")
txtstream.WriteLine("    $txtstream.WriteLine(""    COLOR: white;""')")
txtstream.WriteLine("    $txtstream.WriteLine(""    BACKGROUND-
COLOR: black;""')")
txtstream.WriteLine("    $txtstream.WriteLine(""    FONT-FAMILY:
font-family: Cambria, serif;""')")
```

```
        txtstream.WriteLine("        $txtstream.WriteLine(""        FONT-SIZE:
10px;""")")
        txtstream.WriteLine("        $txtstream.WriteLine(""        text-align:
left;""")")
        txtstream.WriteLine("        $txtstream.WriteLine(""        white-Space:
nowrap;""")")
        txtstream.WriteLine("    $txtstream.WriteLine(""    width: 100%;""")")
        txtstream.WriteLine("    $txtstream.WriteLine(""}""")")
        txtstream.WriteLine("    $txtstream.WriteLine(""select""")")
        txtstream.WriteLine("    $txtstream.WriteLine(""{""")")
        txtstream.WriteLine("    $txtstream.WriteLine(""    COLOR: white;""")")
        txtstream.WriteLine("        $txtstream.WriteLine(""        BACKGROUND-
COLOR: black;""")")
        txtstream.WriteLine("        $txtstream.WriteLine(""        FONT-FAMILY:
font-family: Cambria, serif;""")")
        txtstream.WriteLine("        $txtstream.WriteLine(""        FONT-SIZE:
10px;""")")
        txtstream.WriteLine("        $txtstream.WriteLine(""        text-align:
left;""")")
        txtstream.WriteLine("        $txtstream.WriteLine(""        white-Space:
nowrap;""")")
        txtstream.WriteLine("    $txtstream.WriteLine(""    width: 100%;""")")
        txtstream.WriteLine("    $txtstream.WriteLine(""}""")")
        txtstream.WriteLine("    $txtstream.WriteLine(""input""")")
        txtstream.WriteLine("    $txtstream.WriteLine(""{""")")
        txtstream.WriteLine("    $txtstream.WriteLine(""    COLOR: white;""")")
        txtstream.WriteLine("        $txtstream.WriteLine(""        BACKGROUND-
COLOR: black;""")")
        txtstream.WriteLine("        $txtstream.WriteLine(""        FONT-FAMILY:
font-family: Cambria, serif;""")")
        txtstream.WriteLine("        $txtstream.WriteLine(""        FONT-SIZE:
12px;""")")
        txtstream.WriteLine("        $txtstream.WriteLine(""        text-align:
left;""")")
        txtstream.WriteLine("        $txtstream.WriteLine(""        display:table-
cell;""")")
        txtstream.WriteLine("        $txtstream.WriteLine(""        white-Space:
nowrap;""")")
        txtstream.WriteLine("    $txtstream.WriteLine(""}""")")
        txtstream.WriteLine("    $txtstream.WriteLine(""h1 {""")")
```

```
            txtstream.WriteLine("                $txtstream.WriteLine(""color:
antiquewhite;"")")
            txtstream.WriteLine("        $txtstream.WriteLine(""text-shadow: 1px 1px
1px black;"")")
            txtstream.WriteLine("   $txtstream.WriteLine(""padding: 3px;"")")
            txtstream.WriteLine("                $txtstream.WriteLine(""text-align:
center;"")")
            txtstream.WriteLine("        $txtstream.WriteLine(""box-shadow: in2px
2px 5px rgba(0,0,0,0.5), in-2px -2px 5px rgba(255,255,255,0.5);"")")
            txtstream.WriteLine("   $txtstream.WriteLine(""}"")")
            txtstream.WriteLine("   $txtstream.WriteLine(""</style>"")")


        Case "ColoredText"

            txtstream.WriteLine("                $txtstream.WriteLine(""<style
type='text/css'>"")")
            txtstream.WriteLine("   $txtstream.WriteLine(""th"")")
            txtstream.WriteLine("   $txtstream.WriteLine(""{"")")
            txtstream.WriteLine("            $txtstream.WriteLine(""        COLOR:
darkred;"")")
            txtstream.WriteLine("        $txtstream.WriteLine(""     BACKGROUND-
COLOR: #eeeeee;"")")
            txtstream.WriteLine("            $txtstream.WriteLine(""        FONT-
FAMILY:font-family: Cambria, serif;"")")
            txtstream.WriteLine("        $txtstream.WriteLine(""     FONT-SIZE:
12px;"")")
            txtstream.WriteLine("        $txtstream.WriteLine(""     text-align:
left;"")")
            txtstream.WriteLine("        $txtstream.WriteLine(""     white-Space:
nowrap;"")")
            txtstream.WriteLine("   $txtstream.WriteLine(""}"")")
            txtstream.WriteLine("   $txtstream.WriteLine(""td"")")
            txtstream.WriteLine("   $txtstream.WriteLine(""{"")")
            txtstream.WriteLine("   $txtstream.WriteLine(""   COLOR: navy;"")")
            txtstream.WriteLine("        $txtstream.WriteLine(""     BACKGROUND-
COLOR: #eeeeee;"")")
            txtstream.WriteLine("        $txtstream.WriteLine(""     FONT-FAMILY:
font-family: Cambria, serif;"")")
            txtstream.WriteLine("        $txtstream.WriteLine(""     FONT-SIZE:
12px;"")")
```

```
            txtstream.WriteLine("        $txtstream.WriteLine(""        text-align:
left;"")")
            txtstream.WriteLine("        $txtstream.WriteLine(""        white-Space:
nowrap;"")")
            txtstream.WriteLine("    $txtstream.WriteLine(""}"")")
            txtstream.WriteLine("    $txtstream.WriteLine(""div"")")
            txtstream.WriteLine("    $txtstream.WriteLine(""{"")")
            txtstream.WriteLine("    $txtstream.WriteLine(""    COLOR: white;"")")
            txtstream.WriteLine("        $txtstream.WriteLine(""        BACKGROUND-
COLOR: navy;"")")
            txtstream.WriteLine("        $txtstream.WriteLine(""        FONT-FAMILY:
font-family: Cambria, serif;"")")
            txtstream.WriteLine("        $txtstream.WriteLine(""        FONT-SIZE:
10px;"")")
            txtstream.WriteLine("        $txtstream.WriteLine(""        text-align:
left;"")")
            txtstream.WriteLine("        $txtstream.WriteLine(""        white-Space:
nowrap;"")")
            txtstream.WriteLine("    $txtstream.WriteLine(""}"")")
            txtstream.WriteLine("    $txtstream.WriteLine(""span"")")
            txtstream.WriteLine("    $txtstream.WriteLine(""{"")")
            txtstream.WriteLine("    $txtstream.WriteLine(""    COLOR: white;"")")
            txtstream.WriteLine("        $txtstream.WriteLine(""        BACKGROUND-
COLOR: navy;"")")
            txtstream.WriteLine("        $txtstream.WriteLine(""        FONT-FAMILY:
font-family: Cambria, serif;"")")
            txtstream.WriteLine("        $txtstream.WriteLine(""        FONT-SIZE:
10px;"")")
            txtstream.WriteLine("        $txtstream.WriteLine(""        text-align:
left;"")")
            txtstream.WriteLine("        $txtstream.WriteLine(""        white-Space:
nowrap;"")")
            txtstream.WriteLine("        $txtstream.WriteLine(""        display:inline-
block;"")")
            txtstream.WriteLine("    $txtstream.WriteLine(""    width: 100%;"")")
            txtstream.WriteLine("    $txtstream.WriteLine(""}"")")
            txtstream.WriteLine("    $txtstream.WriteLine(""textarea"")")
            txtstream.WriteLine("    $txtstream.WriteLine(""{"")")
            txtstream.WriteLine("    $txtstream.WriteLine(""    COLOR: white;"")")
```

```
            txtstream.WriteLine("      $txtstream.WriteLine(""        BACKGROUND-
COLOR: navy;"")")
            txtstream.WriteLine("      $txtstream.WriteLine(""        FONT-FAMILY:
font-family: Cambria, serif;"")")
            txtstream.WriteLine("      $txtstream.WriteLine(""        FONT-SIZE:
10px;"")")
            txtstream.WriteLine("      $txtstream.WriteLine(""        text-align:
left;"")")
            txtstream.WriteLine("      $txtstream.WriteLine(""        white-Space:
nowrap;"")")
            txtstream.WriteLine("      $txtstream.WriteLine(""   width: 100%;"")")
            txtstream.WriteLine("      $txtstream.WriteLine(""}"")")
            txtstream.WriteLine("      $txtstream.WriteLine(""select"")")
            txtstream.WriteLine("      $txtstream.WriteLine(""{"")")
            txtstream.WriteLine("      $txtstream.WriteLine(""   COLOR: white;"")")
            txtstream.WriteLine("      $txtstream.WriteLine(""        BACKGROUND-
COLOR: navy;"")")
            txtstream.WriteLine("      $txtstream.WriteLine(""        FONT-FAMILY:
font-family: Cambria, serif;"")")
            txtstream.WriteLine("      $txtstream.WriteLine(""        FONT-SIZE:
10px;"")")
            txtstream.WriteLine("      $txtstream.WriteLine(""        text-align:
left;"")")
            txtstream.WriteLine("      $txtstream.WriteLine(""        white-Space:
nowrap;"")")
            txtstream.WriteLine("      $txtstream.WriteLine(""   width: 100%;"")")
            txtstream.WriteLine("      $txtstream.WriteLine(""}"")")
            txtstream.WriteLine("      $txtstream.WriteLine(""input"")")
            txtstream.WriteLine("      $txtstream.WriteLine(""{"")")
            txtstream.WriteLine("      $txtstream.WriteLine(""   COLOR: white;"")")
            txtstream.WriteLine("      $txtstream.WriteLine(""        BACKGROUND-
COLOR: navy;"")")
            txtstream.WriteLine("      $txtstream.WriteLine(""        FONT-FAMILY:
font-family: Cambria, serif;"")")
            txtstream.WriteLine("      $txtstream.WriteLine(""        FONT-SIZE:
12px;"")")
            txtstream.WriteLine("      $txtstream.WriteLine(""        text-align:
left;"")")
            txtstream.WriteLine("      $txtstream.WriteLine(""        display:table-
cell;"")")
```

```
            txtstream.WriteLine("          $txtstream.WriteLine(""        white-Space:
nowrap;""")")
                txtstream.WriteLine("   $txtstream.WriteLine("""}""")")
                txtstream.WriteLine("   $txtstream.WriteLine("""h1 {""")")
                txtstream.WriteLine("                    $txtstream.WriteLine(""""color:
antiquewhite;""")")
                txtstream.WriteLine("   $txtstream.WriteLine(""""text-shadow: 1px 1px
1px black;""")")
                txtstream.WriteLine("   $txtstream.WriteLine(""""padding: 3px;""")")
                txtstream.WriteLine("              $txtstream.WriteLine(""""text-align:
center;""")")
                txtstream.WriteLine("     $txtstream.WriteLine(""""box-shadow: in2px
2px 5px rgba(0,0,0,0.5), in-2px -2px 5px rgba(255,255,255,0.5);""")")
                txtstream.WriteLine("   $txtstream.WriteLine("""}""")")
                txtstream.WriteLine("   $txtstream.WriteLine(""""</style>""")")


        Case "OscillatingRowColors"


            txtstream.WriteLine("                $txtstream.WriteLine(""""<style
type='text/css'> """)")
                txtstream.WriteLine("   $txtstream.WriteLine(""""th""")")
                txtstream.WriteLine("   $txtstream.WriteLine("""{""")")
                txtstream.WriteLine("   $txtstream.WriteLine(""    COLOR: white;""")")
                txtstream.WriteLine("      $txtstream.WriteLine(""      BACKGROUND-
COLOR: navy;""")")
                txtstream.WriteLine("          $txtstream.WriteLine(""          FONT-
FAMILY:font-family: Cambria, serif;""")")
                txtstream.WriteLine("         $txtstream.WriteLine(""       FONT-SIZE:
12px;""")")
                txtstream.WriteLine("         $txtstream.WriteLine(""        text-align:
left;""")")
                txtstream.WriteLine("         $txtstream.WriteLine(""       white-Space:
nowrap;""")")
                txtstream.WriteLine("   $txtstream.WriteLine("""}""")")
                txtstream.WriteLine("   $txtstream.WriteLine("""td""")")
                txtstream.WriteLine("   $txtstream.WriteLine("""{""")")
                txtstream.WriteLine("   $txtstream.WriteLine(""    COLOR: navy;""")")
```

```
txtstream.WriteLine("                              $txtstream.WriteLine(""        FONT-FAMILY:
font-family: Cambria, serif;"")")
txtstream.WriteLine("                              $txtstream.WriteLine(""        FONT-SIZE:
12px;"")")
txtstream.WriteLine("                              $txtstream.WriteLine(""        text-align:
left;"")")
txtstream.WriteLine("                              $txtstream.WriteLine(""        white-Space:
nowrap;"")")
txtstream.WriteLine("                              $txtstream.WriteLine(""}"")")
txtstream.WriteLine("                              $txtstream.WriteLine(""div"")")
txtstream.WriteLine("                              $txtstream.WriteLine(""{"")")
txtstream.WriteLine("                              $txtstream.WriteLine(""   COLOR: navy;"")")
txtstream.WriteLine("                              $txtstream.WriteLine(""        FONT-FAMILY:
font-family: Cambria, serif;"")")
txtstream.WriteLine("                              $txtstream.WriteLine(""        FONT-SIZE:
12px;"")")
txtstream.WriteLine("                              $txtstream.WriteLine(""        text-align:
left;"")")
txtstream.WriteLine("                              $txtstream.WriteLine(""        white-Space:
nowrap;"")")
txtstream.WriteLine("                              $txtstream.WriteLine(""}"")")
txtstream.WriteLine("                              $txtstream.WriteLine(""span"")")
txtstream.WriteLine("                              $txtstream.WriteLine(""{"")")
txtstream.WriteLine("                              $txtstream.WriteLine(""   COLOR: navy;"")")
txtstream.WriteLine("                              $txtstream.WriteLine(""        FONT-FAMILY:
font-family: Cambria, serif;"")")
txtstream.WriteLine("                              $txtstream.WriteLine(""        FONT-SIZE:
12px;"")")
txtstream.WriteLine("                              $txtstream.WriteLine(""        text-align:
left;"")")
txtstream.WriteLine("                              $txtstream.WriteLine(""        white-Space:
nowrap;"")")
txtstream.WriteLine("                              $txtstream.WriteLine(""   width: 100%;"")")
txtstream.WriteLine("                              $txtstream.WriteLine(""}"")")
txtstream.WriteLine("                              $txtstream.WriteLine(""textarea"")")
txtstream.WriteLine("                              $txtstream.WriteLine(""{"")")
txtstream.WriteLine("                              $txtstream.WriteLine(""   COLOR: navy;"")")
txtstream.WriteLine("                              $txtstream.WriteLine(""        FONT-FAMILY:
font-family: Cambria, serif;"")")
```

```
        txtstream.WriteLine("        $txtstream.WriteLine(""       FONT-SIZE:
12px;"")")
        txtstream.WriteLine("        $txtstream.WriteLine(""       text-align:
left;"")")
        txtstream.WriteLine("        $txtstream.WriteLine(""       white-Space:
nowrap;"")")
        txtstream.WriteLine("        $txtstream.WriteLine(""       display:inline-
block;"")")
        txtstream.WriteLine("        $txtstream.WriteLine(""   width: 100%;"")")
        txtstream.WriteLine("        $txtstream.WriteLine(""}"")")
        txtstream.WriteLine("        $txtstream.WriteLine(""select"")")
        txtstream.WriteLine("        $txtstream.WriteLine(""{"")")
        txtstream.WriteLine("        $txtstream.WriteLine(""   COLOR: navy;"")")
        txtstream.WriteLine("        $txtstream.WriteLine(""       FONT-FAMILY:
font-family: Cambria, serif;"")")
        txtstream.WriteLine("        $txtstream.WriteLine(""       FONT-SIZE:
10px;"")")
        txtstream.WriteLine("        $txtstream.WriteLine(""       text-align:
left;"")")
        txtstream.WriteLine("        $txtstream.WriteLine(""       white-Space:
nowrap;"")")
        txtstream.WriteLine("        $txtstream.WriteLine(""       display:inline-
block;"")")
        txtstream.WriteLine("        $txtstream.WriteLine(""   width: 100%;"")")
        txtstream.WriteLine("        $txtstream.WriteLine(""}"")")
        txtstream.WriteLine("        $txtstream.WriteLine(""input"")")
        txtstream.WriteLine("        $txtstream.WriteLine(""{"")")
        txtstream.WriteLine("        $txtstream.WriteLine(""   COLOR: navy;"")")
        txtstream.WriteLine("        $txtstream.WriteLine(""       FONT-FAMILY:
font-family: Cambria, serif;"")")
        txtstream.WriteLine("        $txtstream.WriteLine(""       FONT-SIZE:
12px;"")")
        txtstream.WriteLine("        $txtstream.WriteLine(""       text-align:
left;"")")
        txtstream.WriteLine("        $txtstream.WriteLine(""       display:table-
cell;"")")
        txtstream.WriteLine("        $txtstream.WriteLine(""       white-Space:
nowrap;"")")
        txtstream.WriteLine("        $txtstream.WriteLine(""}"")")
        txtstream.WriteLine("        $txtstream.WriteLine(""h1 {"")")
```

```
            txtstream.WriteLine("                        $txtstream.WriteLine("""color:
antiquewhite;""")")
            txtstream.WriteLine("    $txtstream.WriteLine("""text-shadow: 1px 1px
1px black;""")")
            txtstream.WriteLine("  $txtstream.WriteLine("""padding: 3px;""")")
            txtstream.WriteLine("                $txtstream.WriteLine("""text-align:
center;""")")
            txtstream.WriteLine("      $txtstream.WriteLine("""box-shadow: in2px
2px 5px rgba(0,0,0,0.5), in-2px -2px 5px rgba(255,255,255,0.5);""")")
            txtstream.WriteLine("  $txtstream.WriteLine("""}""")")
            txtstream.WriteLine("                $txtstream.WriteLine("""tr:nth-
child(even){background-color:#f2f2f2;}""")")
            txtstream.WriteLine("                $txtstream.WriteLine("""tr:nth-
child(odd){background-color:#cccccc; color:#f2f2f2;}""")")
            txtstream.WriteLine("  $txtstream.WriteLine("""</style>""")")


        Case "GhostDecorated"


            txtstream.WriteLine("                    $txtstream.WriteLine("""<style
type='text/css'>""")")
            txtstream.WriteLine("  $txtstream.WriteLine("""th""")")
            txtstream.WriteLine("  $txtstream.WriteLine("""{""")")
            txtstream.WriteLine("  $txtstream.WriteLine(""  COLOR: black;""")")
            txtstream.WriteLine("    $txtstream.WriteLine(""     BACKGROUND-
COLOR: white;""")")
            txtstream.WriteLine("                $txtstream.WriteLine(""     FONT-
FAMILY.font-family: Cambria, scrif;""")")
            txtstream.WriteLine("    $txtstream.WriteLine(""     FONT-SIZE:
12px;""")")
            txtstream.WriteLine("    $txtstream.WriteLine(""     text-align:
left;""")")
            txtstream.WriteLine("    $txtstream.WriteLine(""     white-Space:
nowrap;""")")
            txtstream.WriteLine("  $txtstream.WriteLine("""}""")")
            txtstream.WriteLine("  $txtstream.WriteLine("""td""")")
            txtstream.WriteLine("  $txtstream.WriteLine("""{""")")
            txtstream.WriteLine("  $txtstream.WriteLine(""  COLOR: black;""")")
            txtstream.WriteLine("    $txtstream.WriteLine(""     BACKGROUND-
COLOR: white;""")")
```

```
txtstream.WriteLine("$txtstream.WriteLine("""     FONT-FAMILY: font-family: Cambria, serif;""")")
txtstream.WriteLine("$txtstream.WriteLine("""     FONT-SIZE: 12px;""")")
txtstream.WriteLine("$txtstream.WriteLine("""     text-align: left;""")")
txtstream.WriteLine("$txtstream.WriteLine("""     white-Space: nowrap;""")")
txtstream.WriteLine("$txtstream.WriteLine("""}""")")
txtstream.WriteLine("$txtstream.WriteLine("""div""")")
txtstream.WriteLine("$txtstream.WriteLine"""{""")")
txtstream.WriteLine("$txtstream.WriteLine("""   COLOR: black;""")")
txtstream.WriteLine("$txtstream.WriteLine("""   BACKGROUND-COLOR: white;""")")
txtstream.WriteLine("$txtstream.WriteLine"""   FONT-FAMILY: font-family: Cambria, serif;""")")
txtstream.WriteLine("$txtstream.WriteLine("""   FONT-SIZE: 10px;""")")
txtstream.WriteLine("$txtstream.WriteLine("""   text-align: left;""")")
txtstream.WriteLine("$txtstream.WriteLine("""   white-Space: nowrap;""")")
txtstream.WriteLine("$txtstream.WriteLine("""}""")")
txtstream.WriteLine("$txtstream.WriteLine("""span""")")
txtstream.WriteLine("$txtstream.WriteLine"""{""")")
txtstream.WriteLine("$txtstream.WriteLine("""   COLOR: black;""")")
txtstream.WriteLine("$txtstream.WriteLine("""   BACKGROUND-COLOR: white;""")")
txtstream.WriteLine("$txtstream.WriteLine("""   FONT-FAMILY: font-family: Cambria, serif;""")")
txtstream.WriteLine("$txtstream.WriteLine("""   FONT-SIZE: 10px;""")")
txtstream.WriteLine("$txtstream.WriteLine("""   text-align: left;""")")
txtstream.WriteLine("$txtstream.WriteLine("""   white-Space: nowrap;""")")
txtstream.WriteLine("$txtstream.WriteLine("""   display:inline-block;""")")
txtstream.WriteLine("$txtstream.WriteLine"""   width: 100%;""")")
txtstream.WriteLine("$txtstream.WriteLine("""}""")")
```

```
txtstream.WriteLine("     $txtstream.WriteLine(""""textarea"""")")
txtstream.WriteLine("     $txtstream.WriteLine(""""{"""")")
txtstream.WriteLine("     $txtstream.WriteLine(""""   COLOR: black;"""")")
txtstream.WriteLine("     $txtstream.WriteLine(""""       BACKGROUND-
COLOR: white;"""")")
txtstream.WriteLine("     $txtstream.WriteLine(""""       FONT-FAMILY:
font-family: Cambria, serif;"""")")
txtstream.WriteLine("     $txtstream.WriteLine(""""        FONT-SIZE:
10px;"""")")
txtstream.WriteLine("     $txtstream.WriteLine(""""        text-align:
left;"""")")
txtstream.WriteLine("     $txtstream.WriteLine(""""        white-Space:
nowrap;"""")")
txtstream.WriteLine("     $txtstream.WriteLine(""""   width: 100%;"""")")
txtstream.WriteLine("     $txtstream.WriteLine(""""}"""")")
txtstream.WriteLine("     $txtstream.WriteLine(""""select"""")")
txtstream.WriteLine("     $txtstream.WriteLine(""""{"""")")
txtstream.WriteLine("     $txtstream.WriteLine(""""   COLOR: black;"""")")
txtstream.WriteLine("     $txtstream.WriteLine(""""       BACKGROUND-
COLOR: white;"""")")
txtstream.WriteLine("     $txtstream.WriteLine(""""       FONT-FAMILY:
font-family: Cambria, serif;"""")")
txtstream.WriteLine("     $txtstream.WriteLine(""""        FONT-SIZE:
10px;"""")")
txtstream.WriteLine("     $txtstream.WriteLine(""""        text-align:
left;"""")")
txtstream.WriteLine("     $txtstream.WriteLine(""""        white-Space:
nowrap;"""")")
txtstream.WriteLine("     $txtstream.WriteLine(""""   width: 100%;"""")")
txtstream.WriteLine("     $txtstream.WriteLine(""""}"""")")
txtstream.WriteLine("     $txtstream.WriteLine(""""input"""")")
txtstream.WriteLine("     $txtstream.WriteLine(""""{"""")")
txtstream.WriteLine("     $txtstream.WriteLine(""""   COLOR: black;"""")")
txtstream.WriteLine("     $txtstream.WriteLine(""""       BACKGROUND-
COLOR: white;"""")")
txtstream.WriteLine("     $txtstream.WriteLine(""""       FONT-FAMILY:
font-family: Cambria, serif;"""")")
txtstream.WriteLine("     $txtstream.WriteLine(""""        FONT-SIZE:
12px;"""")")
```

```
            txtstream.WriteLine("        $txtstream.WriteLine(""        text-align:
left;"")")
            txtstream.WriteLine("        $txtstream.WriteLine(""        display:table-
cell;"")")
            txtstream.WriteLine("        $txtstream.WriteLine(""        white-Space:
nowrap;"")")
            txtstream.WriteLine("    $txtstream.WriteLine(""}"")")
            txtstream.WriteLine("    $txtstream.WriteLine(""h1 {"")")
            txtstream.WriteLine("                $txtstream.WriteLine(""color:
antiquewhite;"")")
            txtstream.WriteLine("        $txtstream.WriteLine(""text-shadow: 1px 1px
1px black;"")")
            txtstream.WriteLine("    $txtstream.WriteLine(""padding: 3px;"")")
            txtstream.WriteLine("            $txtstream.WriteLine(""text-align:
center;"")")
            txtstream.WriteLine("    $txtstream.WriteLine(""box-shadow: in2px
2px 5px rgba(0,0,0,0.5), in-2px -2px 5px rgba(255,255,255,0.5);"")")
            txtstream.WriteLine("    $txtstream.WriteLine(""}"")")
            txtstream.WriteLine("    $txtstream.WriteLine(""</style>"")")


        Case "3D"


            txtstream.WriteLine("                $txtstream.WriteLine(""<style
type='text/css'>"")")
            txtstream.WriteLine("    $txtstream.WriteLine(""body"")")
            txtstream.WriteLine("    $txtstream.WriteLine(""{"")")
            txtstream.WriteLine("        $txtstream.WriteLine(""    PADDING-RIGHT:
0px;"")")
            txtstream.WriteLine("        $txtstream.WriteLine(""    PADDING-LEFT:
0px;"")")
            txtstream.WriteLine("            $txtstream.WriteLine(""    PADDING-
BOTTOM: 0px;"")")
            txtstream.WriteLine("    $txtstream.WriteLine(""    MARGIN: 0px;"")")
            txtstream.WriteLine("    $txtstream.WriteLine(""    COLOR: #333;"")")
            txtstream.WriteLine("        $txtstream.WriteLine(""    PADDING-TOP:
0px;"")")
            txtstream.WriteLine("        $txtstream.WriteLine(""    FONT-FAMILY:
verdana, arial, helvetica, sans-serif;"")")
            txtstream.WriteLine("    $txtstream.WriteLine(""}"")")
```

```
txtstream.WriteLine("    $txtstream.WriteLine("""table""")")
txtstream.WriteLine("    $txtstream.WriteLine("""{""")")
txtstream.WriteLine("    $txtstream.WriteLine("""    BORDER-RIGHT:
#999999 3px solid;""")")
txtstream.WriteLine("    $txtstream.WriteLine("""    PADDING-RIGHT:
6px;""")")
txtstream.WriteLine("    $txtstream.WriteLine("""    PADDING-LEFT:
6px;""")")
txtstream.WriteLine("    $txtstream.WriteLine("""    FONT-WEIGHT:
Bold;""")")
txtstream.WriteLine("    $txtstream.WriteLine("""    FONT-SIZE:
14px;""")")
txtstream.WriteLine("    $txtstream.WriteLine("""    PADDING-
BOTTOM: 6px;""")")
txtstream.WriteLine("    $txtstream.WriteLine("""    COLOR: Peru;""")")
txtstream.WriteLine("    $txtstream.WriteLine("""    LINE-HEIGHT:
14px;""")")
txtstream.WriteLine("    $txtstream.WriteLine("""    PADDING-TOP:
6px;""")")
txtstream.WriteLine("    $txtstream.WriteLine("""    BORDER-BOTTOM:
#999 1px solid;""")")
txtstream.WriteLine("    $txtstream.WriteLine("""    BACKGROUND-
COLOR: #eeeeee;""")")
txtstream.WriteLine("    $txtstream.WriteLine("""    FONT-FAMILY:
verdana, arial, helvetica, sans-serif;""")")
txtstream.WriteLine("    $txtstream.WriteLine("""    FONT-SIZE:
12px;""")")
txtstream.WriteLine("    $txtstream.WriteLine("""}""")")
txtstream.WriteLine("    $txtstream.WriteLine("""th""")")
txtstream.WriteLine("    $txtstream.WriteLine("""{""")")
txtstream.WriteLine("    $txtstream.WriteLine("""    BORDER-RIGHT:
#999999 3px solid;""")")
txtstream.WriteLine("    $txtstream.WriteLine("""    PADDING-RIGHT:
6px;""")")
txtstream.WriteLine("    $txtstream.WriteLine("""    PADDING-LEFT:
6px;""")")
txtstream.WriteLine("    $txtstream.WriteLine("""    FONT-WEIGHT:
Bold;""")")
txtstream.WriteLine("    $txtstream.WriteLine("""    FONT-SIZE:
14px;""")")
```

```
            txtstream.WriteLine("      $txtstream.WriteLine(""        PADDING-
BOTTOM: 6px;"")")
            txtstream.WriteLine("          $txtstream.WriteLine(""          COLOR:
darkred;"")")
            txtstream.WriteLine("      $txtstream.WriteLine(""      LINE-HEIGHT:
14px;"")")
            txtstream.WriteLine("      $txtstream.WriteLine(""      PADDING-TOP:
6px;"")")
            txtstream.WriteLine("    $txtstream.WriteLine(""    BORDER-BOTTOM:
#999 1px solid;"")")
            txtstream.WriteLine("    $txtstream.WriteLine(""    BACKGROUND-
COLOR: #eeeeee;"")")
            txtstream.WriteLine("          $txtstream.WriteLine(""          FONT-
FAMILY:font-family: Cambria, serif;"")")
            txtstream.WriteLine("      $txtstream.WriteLine(""      FONT-SIZE:
12px;"")")
            txtstream.WriteLine("      $txtstream.WriteLine(""      text-align:
left;"")")
            txtstream.WriteLine("      $txtstream.WriteLine(""      white-Space:
nowrap;"")")
            txtstream.WriteLine("  $txtstream.WriteLine(""}"")")
            txtstream.WriteLine("  $txtstream.WriteLine("".th"")")
            txtstream.WriteLine("  $txtstream.WriteLine(""{"")")
            txtstream.WriteLine("    $txtstream.WriteLine(""    BORDER-RIGHT:
#999999 2px solid;"")")
            txtstream.WriteLine("    $txtstream.WriteLine(""    PADDING-RIGHT:
6px;"")")
            txtstream.WriteLine("    $txtstream.WriteLine(""    PADDING-LEFT:
6px;"")")
            txtstream.WriteLine("    $txtstream.WriteLine(""    FONT-WEIGHT:
Bold;"")")
            txtstream.WriteLine("      $txtstream.WriteLine(""      PADDING-
BOTTOM: 6px;"")")
            txtstream.WriteLine("  $txtstream.WriteLine(""  COLOR: black;"")")
            txtstream.WriteLine("    $txtstream.WriteLine(""    PADDING-TOP:
6px;"")")
            txtstream.WriteLine("  $txtstream.WriteLine(""  BORDER-BOTTOM:
#999 2px solid;"")")
            txtstream.WriteLine("    $txtstream.WriteLine(""    BACKGROUND-
COLOR: #eeeeee;"")")
```

```
           txtstream.WriteLine("              $txtstream.WriteLine(""        FONT-FAMILY:
font-family: Cambria, serif;""")")
           txtstream.WriteLine("              $txtstream.WriteLine(""        FONT-SIZE:
10px;""")")
           txtstream.WriteLine("              $txtstream.WriteLine(""        text-align:
right;""")")
           txtstream.WriteLine("              $txtstream.WriteLine(""        white-Space:
nowrap;""")")
           txtstream.WriteLine("         $txtstream.WriteLine(""}""")")
           txtstream.WriteLine("         $txtstream.WriteLine(""td""")")
           txtstream.WriteLine("         $txtstream.WriteLine(""{""")")
           txtstream.WriteLine("              $txtstream.WriteLine(""        BORDER-RIGHT:
#999999 3px solid;""")")
           txtstream.WriteLine("              $txtstream.WriteLine(""        PADDING-RIGHT:
6px;""")")
           txtstream.WriteLine("              $txtstream.WriteLine(""        PADDING-LEFT:
6px;""")")
           txtstream.WriteLine("              $txtstream.WriteLine(""        FONT-WEIGHT:
Normal;""")")
           txtstream.WriteLine("              $txtstream.WriteLine(""        PADDING-
BOTTOM: 6px;""")")
           txtstream.WriteLine("         $txtstream.WriteLine(""    COLOR: navy;""")")
           txtstream.WriteLine("              $txtstream.WriteLine(""        LINE-HEIGHT:
14px;""")")
           txtstream.WriteLine("              $txtstream.WriteLine(""        PADDING-TOP:
6px;""")")
           txtstream.WriteLine("         $txtstream.WriteLine(""    BORDER-BOTTOM:
#999 1px solid;""")")
           txtstream.WriteLine("              $txtstream.WriteLine(""        BACKGROUND-
COLOR: #eeeeee;""")")
           txtstream.WriteLine("              $txtstream.WriteLine(""        FONT-FAMILY:
font-family: Cambria, serif;""")")
           txtstream.WriteLine("              $txtstream.WriteLine(""        FONT-SIZE:
12px;""")")
           txtstream.WriteLine("              $txtstream.WriteLine(""        text-align:
left;""")")
           txtstream.WriteLine("              $txtstream.WriteLine(""        white-Space:
nowrap;""")")
           txtstream.WriteLine("         $txtstream.WriteLine(""}""")")
           txtstream.WriteLine("         $txtstream.WriteLine(""div""")")
```

```
        txtstream.WriteLine("    $txtstream.WriteLine(""""{""")")
        txtstream.WriteLine("    $txtstream.WriteLine(""""    BORDER-RIGHT:
#999999 3px solid;""")")
        txtstream.WriteLine("    $txtstream.WriteLine(""""    PADDING-RIGHT:
6px;""")")
        txtstream.WriteLine("    $txtstream.WriteLine(""""    PADDING-LEFT:
6px;""")")
        txtstream.WriteLine("    $txtstream.WriteLine(""""    FONT-WEIGHT:
Normal;""")")
        txtstream.WriteLine("    $txtstream.WriteLine(""""    PADDING-
BOTTOM: 6px;""")")
        txtstream.WriteLine("    $txtstream.WriteLine(""""    COLOR: white;""")")
        txtstream.WriteLine("    $txtstream.WriteLine(""""    PADDING-TOP:
6px;""")")
        txtstream.WriteLine("    $txtstream.WriteLine(""""    BORDER-BOTTOM:
#999 1px solid;""")")
        txtstream.WriteLine("    $txtstream.WriteLine(""""    BACKGROUND-
COLOR: navy;""")")
        txtstream.WriteLine("    $txtstream.WriteLine(""""    FONT-FAMILY:
font-family: Cambria, serif;""")")
        txtstream.WriteLine("    $txtstream.WriteLine(""""    FONT-SIZE:
10px;""")")
        txtstream.WriteLine("    $txtstream.WriteLine(""""    text-align:
left;""")")
        txtstream.WriteLine("    $txtstream.WriteLine(""""    white-Space:
nowrap;""")")
        txtstream.WriteLine("    $txtstream.WriteLine(""""}""")")
        txtstream.WriteLine("    $txtstream.WriteLine(""""span""")")
        txtstream.WriteLine("    $txtstream.WriteLine(""""{""")")
        txtstream.WriteLine("    $txtstream.WriteLine(""""    BORDER-RIGHT:
#999999 3px solid;""")")
        txtstream.WriteLine("    $txtstream.WriteLine(""""    PADDING-RIGHT:
3px;""")")
        txtstream.WriteLine("    $txtstream.WriteLine(""""    PADDING-LEFT:
3px;""")")
        txtstream.WriteLine("    $txtstream.WriteLine(""""    FONT-WEIGHT:
Normal;""")")
        txtstream.WriteLine("    $txtstream.WriteLine(""""    PADDING-
BOTTOM: 3px;""")")
        txtstream.WriteLine("    $txtstream.WriteLine(""""    COLOR: white;""")")
```

```
txtstream.WriteLine("              $txtstream.WriteLine(""        PADDING-TOP:
3px;""")")

txtstream.WriteLine("              $txtstream.WriteLine(""        BORDER-BOTTOM:
#999 1px solid;""")")

txtstream.WriteLine("              $txtstream.WriteLine(""        BACKGROUND-
COLOR: navy;""")")

txtstream.WriteLine("              $txtstream.WriteLine(""        FONT-FAMILY:
font-family: Cambria, serif;""")")

txtstream.WriteLine("              $txtstream.WriteLine(""          FONT-SIZE:
10px;""")")

txtstream.WriteLine("              $txtstream.WriteLine(""          text-align:
left;""")")

txtstream.WriteLine("              $txtstream.WriteLine(""          white-Space:
nowrap;""")")

txtstream.WriteLine("              $txtstream.WriteLine(""          display:inline-
block;""")")

txtstream.WriteLine("              $txtstream.WriteLine(""    width: 100%;""")")
txtstream.WriteLine("              $txtstream.WriteLine(""}""")")
txtstream.WriteLine("              $txtstream.WriteLine(""textarea""")")
txtstream.WriteLine("              $txtstream.WriteLine(""{""")")
txtstream.WriteLine("              $txtstream.WriteLine(""        BORDER-RIGHT:
#999999 3px solid;""")")

txtstream.WriteLine("              $txtstream.WriteLine(""        PADDING-RIGHT:
3px;""")")

txtstream.WriteLine("              $txtstream.WriteLine(""        PADDING-LEFT:
3px;""")")

txtstream.WriteLine("              $txtstream.WriteLine(""        FONT-WEIGHT:
Normal;""")")

txtstream.WriteLine("              $txtstream.WriteLine(""          PADDING-
BOTTOM: 3px;""")")

txtstream.WriteLine("              $txtstream.WriteLine(""    COLOR: white;""")")
txtstream.WriteLine("              $txtstream.WriteLine(""        PADDING-TOP:
3px;""")")

txtstream.WriteLine("              $txtstream.WriteLine(""        BORDER-BOTTOM:
#999 1px solid;""")")

txtstream.WriteLine("              $txtstream.WriteLine(""        BACKGROUND-
COLOR: navy;""")")

txtstream.WriteLine("              $txtstream.WriteLine(""        FONT-FAMILY:
font-family: Cambria, serif;""")")
```

```
            txtstream.WriteLine("        $txtstream.WriteLine(""        FONT-SIZE:
10px;"")")
            txtstream.WriteLine("        $txtstream.WriteLine(""        text-align:
left;"")")
            txtstream.WriteLine("        $txtstream.WriteLine(""        white-Space:
nowrap;"")")
            txtstream.WriteLine("    $txtstream.WriteLine(""   width: 100%;"")")
            txtstream.WriteLine("    $txtstream.WriteLine(""}"")")
            txtstream.WriteLine("    $txtstream.WriteLine(""select"")")
            txtstream.WriteLine("    $txtstream.WriteLine(""{"")")
            txtstream.WriteLine("        $txtstream.WriteLine(""        BORDER-RIGHT:
#999999 3px solid;"")")
            txtstream.WriteLine("        $txtstream.WriteLine(""        PADDING-RIGHT:
6px;"")")
            txtstream.WriteLine("        $txtstream.WriteLine(""        PADDING-LEFT:
6px;"")")
            txtstream.WriteLine("        $txtstream.WriteLine(""        FONT-WEIGHT:
Normal;"")")
            txtstream.WriteLine("        $txtstream.WriteLine(""        PADDING-
BOTTOM: 6px;"")")
            txtstream.WriteLine("    $txtstream.WriteLine(""    COLOR: white;"")")
            txtstream.WriteLine("        $txtstream.WriteLine(""        PADDING-TOP:
6px;"")")
            txtstream.WriteLine("        $txtstream.WriteLine(""        BORDER-BOTTOM:
#999 1px solid;"")")
            txtstream.WriteLine("        $txtstream.WriteLine(""        BACKGROUND-
COLOR: navy;"")")
            txtstream.WriteLine("        $txtstream.WriteLine(""        FONT-FAMILY:
font-family: Cambria, serif;"")")
            txtstream.WriteLine("        $txtstream.WriteLine(""        FONT-SIZE:
10px;"")")
            txtstream.WriteLine("        $txtstream.WriteLine(""        text-align:
left;"")")
            txtstream.WriteLine("        $txtstream.WriteLine(""        white-Space:
nowrap;"")")
            txtstream.WriteLine("    $txtstream.WriteLine(""   width: 100%;"")")
            txtstream.WriteLine("    $txtstream.WriteLine(""}"")")
            txtstream.WriteLine("    $txtstream.WriteLine(""input"")")
            txtstream.WriteLine("    $txtstream.WriteLine(""{"")")
```

```
        txtstream.WriteLine("        $txtstream.WriteLine(""    BORDER-RIGHT:
#999999 3px solid;"")")
        txtstream.WriteLine("        $txtstream.WriteLine(""    PADDING-RIGHT:
3px;"")")
        txtstream.WriteLine("        $txtstream.WriteLine(""    PADDING-LEFT:
3px;"")")
        txtstream.WriteLine("        $txtstream.WriteLine(""    FONT-WEIGHT:
Bold;"")")
        txtstream.WriteLine("        $txtstream.WriteLine(""    PADDING-
BOTTOM: 3px;"")")
        txtstream.WriteLine("        $txtstream.WriteLine(""    COLOR: white;"")")
        txtstream.WriteLine("        $txtstream.WriteLine(""    PADDING-TOP:
3px;"")")
        txtstream.WriteLine("        $txtstream.WriteLine(""    BORDER-BOTTOM:
#999 1px solid;"")")
        txtstream.WriteLine("        $txtstream.WriteLine(""    BACKGROUND-
COLOR: navy;"")")
        txtstream.WriteLine("        $txtstream.WriteLine(""    FONT-FAMILY:
font-family: Cambria, serif;"")")
        txtstream.WriteLine("        $txtstream.WriteLine(""    FONT-SIZE:
12px;"")")
        txtstream.WriteLine("        $txtstream.WriteLine(""    text-align:
left;"")")
        txtstream.WriteLine("        $txtstream.WriteLine(""    display:table-
cell;"")")
        txtstream.WriteLine("        $txtstream.WriteLine(""    white-Space:
nowrap;"")")
        txtstream.WriteLine("        $txtstream.WriteLine(""    width: 100%;"")")
        txtstream.WriteLine("        $txtstream.WriteLine(""}"")")
        txtstream.WriteLine("        $txtstream.WriteLine(""h1 {"")")
        txtstream.WriteLine("        $txtstream.WriteLine(""color:
antiquewhite;"")")
        txtstream.WriteLine("        $txtstream.WriteLine(""text-shadow: 1px 1px
1px black;"")")
        txtstream.WriteLine("        $txtstream.WriteLine(""padding: 3px;"")")
        txtstream.WriteLine("        $txtstream.WriteLine(""text-align:
center;"")")
        txtstream.WriteLine("        $txtstream.WriteLine(""box-shadow: in2px
2px 5px rgba(0,0,0,0.5), in-2px -2px 5px rgba(255,255,255,0.5);"")")
        txtstream.WriteLine("        $txtstream.WriteLine(""}"")")
```

```
            txtstream.WriteLine("    $txtstream.WriteLine(""</style>"")")

        Case "ShadowBox"

            txtstream.WriteLine("                    $txtstream.WriteLine(""<style
type='text/css'>"")")
            txtstream.WriteLine("    $txtstream.WriteLine(""body"")")
            txtstream.WriteLine("    $txtstream.WriteLine(""{"")")
            txtstream.WriteLine("    $txtstream.WriteLine(""    PADDING-RIGHT:
0px;"")")
            txtstream.WriteLine("    $txtstream.WriteLine(""    PADDING-LEFT:
0px;"")")
            txtstream.WriteLine("    $txtstream.WriteLine(""    PADDING-
BOTTOM: 0px;"")")
            txtstream.WriteLine("    $txtstream.WriteLine(""    MARGIN: 0px;"")")
            txtstream.WriteLine("    $txtstream.WriteLine(""    COLOR: #333;"")")
            txtstream.WriteLine("    $txtstream.WriteLine(""    PADDING-TOP:
0px;"")")
            txtstream.WriteLine("    $txtstream.WriteLine(""    FONT-FAMILY:
verdana, arial, helvetica, sans-serif;"")")
            txtstream.WriteLine("    $txtstream.WriteLine(""}"")")
            txtstream.WriteLine("    $txtstream.WriteLine(""table"")")
            txtstream.WriteLine("    $txtstream.WriteLine(""{"")")
            txtstream.WriteLine("    $txtstream.WriteLine(""    BORDER-RIGHT:
#999999 1px solid;"")")
            txtstream.WriteLine("    $txtstream.WriteLine(""    PADDING-RIGHT:
1px;"")")
            txtstream.WriteLine("    $txtstream.WriteLine(""    PADDING-LEFT:
1px;"")")
            txtstream.WriteLine("    $txtstream.WriteLine(""    PADDING-
BOTTOM: 1px;"")")
            txtstream.WriteLine("    $txtstream.WriteLine(""    LINE-HEIGHT:
8px;"")")
            txtstream.WriteLine("    $txtstream.WriteLine(""    PADDING-TOP:
1px;"")")
            txtstream.WriteLine("    $txtstream.WriteLine(""    BORDER-BOTTOM:
#999 1px solid;"")")
            txtstream.WriteLine("    $txtstream.WriteLine(""    BACKGROUND-
COLOR: #eeeeee;"")")
```

```
        txtstream.WriteLine("                        $txtstream.WriteLine(""
filter:progid:DXImageTransform.Microsoft.Shadow(color='silver',        Direction=135,
Strength=16)"")")
            txtstream.WriteLine("    $txtstream.WriteLine(""}"")")
            txtstream.WriteLine("    $txtstream.WriteLine(""th"")")
            txtstream.WriteLine("    $txtstream.WriteLine(""{"")")
            txtstream.WriteLine("    $txtstream.WriteLine(""    BORDER-RIGHT:
#999999 3px solid;"")")
            txtstream.WriteLine("    $txtstream.WriteLine(""    PADDING-RIGHT:
6px;"")")
            txtstream.WriteLine("    $txtstream.WriteLine(""    PADDING-LEFT:
6px;"")")
            txtstream.WriteLine("    $txtstream.WriteLine(""    FONT-WEIGHT:
Bold;"")")
            txtstream.WriteLine("    $txtstream.WriteLine(""    FONT-SIZE:
14px;"")")
            txtstream.WriteLine("    $txtstream.WriteLine(""    PADDING-
BOTTOM: 6px;"")")
            txtstream.WriteLine("    $txtstream.WriteLine(""    COLOR:
darkred;"")")
            txtstream.WriteLine("    $txtstream.WriteLine(""    LINE-HEIGHT:
14px;"")")
            txtstream.WriteLine("    $txtstream.WriteLine(""    PADDING-TOP:
6px;"")")
            txtstream.WriteLine("    $txtstream.WriteLine(""    BORDER-BOTTOM:
#999 1px solid;"")")
            txtstream.WriteLine("    $txtstream.WriteLine(""    BACKGROUND-
COLOR: #eeeeee;"")")
            txtstream.WriteLine("    $txtstream.WriteLine(""    FONT-FAMILY:
font-family: Cambria, serif;"")")
            txtstream.WriteLine("    $txtstream.WriteLine(""    FONT-SIZE:
12px;"")")
            txtstream.WriteLine("    $txtstream.WriteLine(""    text-align:
left;"")")
            txtstream.WriteLine("    $txtstream.WriteLine(""    white-Space:
nowrap;"")")
            txtstream.WriteLine("    $txtstream.WriteLine(""}"")")
            txtstream.WriteLine("    $txtstream.WriteLine("".th"")")
            txtstream.WriteLine("    $txtstream.WriteLine(""{"")")
```

```
            txtstream.WriteLine("    $txtstream.WriteLine(""    BORDER-RIGHT:
#999999 2px solid;"")")
            txtstream.WriteLine("    $txtstream.WriteLine(""    PADDING-RIGHT:
6px;"")")
            txtstream.WriteLine("    $txtstream.WriteLine(""    PADDING-LEFT:
6px;"")")
            txtstream.WriteLine("    $txtstream.WriteLine(""    FONT-WEIGHT:
Bold;"")")
            txtstream.WriteLine("    $txtstream.WriteLine(""    PADDING-
BOTTOM: 6px;"")")
            txtstream.WriteLine("    $txtstream.WriteLine(""    COLOR: black;"")")
            txtstream.WriteLine("    $txtstream.WriteLine(""    PADDING-TOP:
6px;"")")
            txtstream.WriteLine("    $txtstream.WriteLine(""    BORDER-BOTTOM:
#999 2px solid;"")")
            txtstream.WriteLine("    $txtstream.WriteLine(""    BACKGROUND-
COLOR: #eeeeee;"")")
            txtstream.WriteLine("    $txtstream.WriteLine(""    FONT-FAMILY:
font-family: Cambria, serif;"")")
            txtstream.WriteLine("    $txtstream.WriteLine(""    FONT-SIZE:
10px;"")")
            txtstream.WriteLine("    $txtstream.WriteLine(""    text-align:
right;"")")
            txtstream.WriteLine("    $txtstream.WriteLine(""    white-Space:
nowrap;"")")
            txtstream.WriteLine("    $txtstream.WriteLine(""}"")")
            txtstream.WriteLine("    $txtstream.WriteLine(""td"")")
            txtstream.WriteLine("    $txtstream.WriteLine(""{"")")
            txtstream.WriteLine("    $txtstream.WriteLine(""    BORDER-RIGHT:
#999999 3px solid;"")")
            txtstream.WriteLine("    $txtstream.WriteLine(""    PADDING-RIGHT:
6px;"")")
            txtstream.WriteLine("    $txtstream.WriteLine(""    PADDING-LEFT:
6px;"")")
            txtstream.WriteLine("    $txtstream.WriteLine(""    FONT-WEIGHT:
Normal;"")")
            txtstream.WriteLine("    $txtstream.WriteLine(""    PADDING-
BOTTOM: 6px;"")")
            txtstream.WriteLine("    $txtstream.WriteLine(""    COLOR: navy;"")")
```

```
txtstream.WriteLine("          $txtstream.WriteLine(""      LINE-HEIGHT:
14px;""")")
txtstream.WriteLine("          $txtstream.WriteLine(""      PADDING-TOP:
6px;""")")
txtstream.WriteLine("          $txtstream.WriteLine(""      BORDER-BOTTOM:
#999 1px solid;""")")
txtstream.WriteLine("          $txtstream.WriteLine(""      BACKGROUND-
COLOR: #eeeeee;""")")
txtstream.WriteLine("          $txtstream.WriteLine(""      FONT-FAMILY:
font-family: Cambria, serif;""")")
txtstream.WriteLine("          $txtstream.WriteLine(""      FONT-SIZE:
12px;""")")
txtstream.WriteLine("          $txtstream.WriteLine(""      text-align:
left;""")")
txtstream.WriteLine("          $txtstream.WriteLine(""      white-Space:
nowrap;""")")
txtstream.WriteLine("          $txtstream.WriteLine(""}""")")
txtstream.WriteLine("          $txtstream.WriteLine(""div""")")
txtstream.WriteLine("          $txtstream.WriteLine(""{""")")
txtstream.WriteLine("          $txtstream.WriteLine(""      BORDER-RIGHT:
#999999 3px solid;""")")
txtstream.WriteLine("          $txtstream.WriteLine(""      PADDING-RIGHT:
6px;""")")
txtstream.WriteLine("          $txtstream.WriteLine(""      PADDING-LEFT:
6px;""")")
txtstream.WriteLine("          $txtstream.WriteLine(""      FONT-WEIGHT:
Normal;""")")
txtstream.WriteLine("          $txtstream.WriteLine(""      PADDING-
BOTTOM: 6px;""")")
txtstream.WriteLine("          $txtstream.WriteLine(""    COLOR: white;""")")
txtstream.WriteLine("          $txtstream.WriteLine(""      PADDING-TOP:
6px;""")")
txtstream.WriteLine("          $txtstream.WriteLine(""      BORDER-BOTTOM:
#999 1px solid;""")")
txtstream.WriteLine("          $txtstream.WriteLine(""      BACKGROUND-
COLOR: navy;""")")
txtstream.WriteLine("          $txtstream.WriteLine(""      FONT-FAMILY:
font-family: Cambria, serif;""")")
txtstream.WriteLine("          $txtstream.WriteLine(""      FONT-SIZE:
10px;""")")
```

```
            txtstream.WriteLine("          $txtstream.WriteLine(""          text-align:
left;"")")
            txtstream.WriteLine("          $txtstream.WriteLine(""          white-Space:
nowrap;"")")
            txtstream.WriteLine("     $txtstream.WriteLine(""}"")")
            txtstream.WriteLine("     $txtstream.WriteLine(""span"")")
            txtstream.WriteLine("     $txtstream.WriteLine(""{"")")
            txtstream.WriteLine("     $txtstream.WriteLine(""     BORDER-RIGHT:
#999999 3px solid;"")")
            txtstream.WriteLine("     $txtstream.WriteLine(""     PADDING-RIGHT:
3px;"")")
            txtstream.WriteLine("     $txtstream.WriteLine(""     PADDING-LEFT:
3px;"")")
            txtstream.WriteLine("     $txtstream.WriteLine(""     FONT-WEIGHT:
Normal;"")")
            txtstream.WriteLine("     $txtstream.WriteLine(""     PADDING-
BOTTOM: 3px;"")")
            txtstream.WriteLine("     $txtstream.WriteLine(""   COLOR: white;"")")
            txtstream.WriteLine("     $txtstream.WriteLine(""     PADDING-TOP:
3px;"")")
            txtstream.WriteLine("     $txtstream.WriteLine(""     BORDER-BOTTOM:
#999 1px solid;"")")
            txtstream.WriteLine("     $txtstream.WriteLine(""     BACKGROUND-
COLOR: navy;"")")
            txtstream.WriteLine("     $txtstream.WriteLine(""     FONT-FAMILY:
font-family: Cambria, serif;"")")
            txtstream.WriteLine("     $txtstream.WriteLine(""     FONT-SIZE:
10px;"")")
            txtstream.WriteLine("     $txtstream.WriteLine(""     text-align:
left;"")")
            txtstream.WriteLine("     $txtstream.WriteLine(""     white-Space:
nowrap;"")")
            txtstream.WriteLine("     $txtstream.WriteLine(""     display: inline-
block;"")")
            txtstream.WriteLine("     $txtstream.WriteLine(""   width: 100%;"")")
            txtstream.WriteLine("     $txtstream.WriteLine(""}"")")
            txtstream.WriteLine("     $txtstream.WriteLine(""textarea"")")
            txtstream.WriteLine("     $txtstream.WriteLine(""{"")")
            txtstream.WriteLine("     $txtstream.WriteLine(""     BORDER-RIGHT:
#999999 3px solid;"")")
```

```
        txtstream.WriteLine("    $txtstream.WriteLine(""    PADDING-RIGHT:
3px;"")")
        txtstream.WriteLine("    $txtstream.WriteLine(""    PADDING-LEFT:
3px;"")")
        txtstream.WriteLine("    $txtstream.WriteLine(""    FONT-WEIGHT:
Normal;"")")
        txtstream.WriteLine("    $txtstream.WriteLine(""    PADDING-
BOTTOM: 3px;"")")
        txtstream.WriteLine("    $txtstream.WriteLine(""    COLOR: white;"")")
        txtstream.WriteLine("    $txtstream.WriteLine(""    PADDING-TOP:
3px;"")")
        txtstream.WriteLine("    $txtstream.WriteLine(""    BORDER-BOTTOM:
#999 1px solid;"")")
        txtstream.WriteLine("    $txtstream.WriteLine(""    BACKGROUND-
COLOR: navy;"")")
        txtstream.WriteLine("    $txtstream.WriteLine(""    FONT-FAMILY:
font-family: Cambria, serif;"")")
        txtstream.WriteLine("    $txtstream.WriteLine(""    FONT-SIZE:
10px;"")")
        txtstream.WriteLine("    $txtstream.WriteLine(""    text-align:
left;"")")
        txtstream.WriteLine("    $txtstream.WriteLine(""    white-Space:
nowrap;"")")
        txtstream.WriteLine("    $txtstream.WriteLine(""    width: 100%;"")")
        txtstream.WriteLine("    $txtstream.WriteLine(""}"")")
        txtstream.WriteLine("    $txtstream.WriteLine(""select"")")
        txtstream.WriteLine("    $txtstream.WriteLine(""{"")")
        txtstream.WriteLine("    $txtstream.WriteLine(""    BORDER-RIGHT:
#999999 3px solid;"")")
        txtstream.WriteLine("    $txtstream.WriteLine(""    PADDING-RIGHT:
6px;"")")
        txtstream.WriteLine("    $txtstream.WriteLine(""    PADDING-LEFT:
6px;"")")
        txtstream.WriteLine("    $txtstream.WriteLine(""    FONT-WEIGHT:
Normal;"")")
        txtstream.WriteLine("    $txtstream.WriteLine(""    PADDING-
BOTTOM: 6px;"")")
        txtstream.WriteLine("    $txtstream.WriteLine(""    COLOR: white;"")")
        txtstream.WriteLine("    $txtstream.WriteLine(""    PADDING-TOP:
6px;"")")
```

```
            txtstream.WriteLine("    $txtstream.WriteLine(""    BORDER-BOTTOM: #999 1px solid;""")")
            txtstream.WriteLine("    $txtstream.WriteLine(""    BACKGROUND-COLOR: navy;""")")
            txtstream.WriteLine("    $txtstream.WriteLine(""    FONT-FAMILY: font-family: Cambria, serif;""")")
            txtstream.WriteLine("    $txtstream.WriteLine(""    FONT-SIZE: 10px;""")")
            txtstream.WriteLine("    $txtstream.WriteLine(""    text-align: left;""")")
            txtstream.WriteLine("    $txtstream.WriteLine(""    white-Space: nowrap;""")")
            txtstream.WriteLine("    $txtstream.WriteLine(""  width: 100%;""")")
            txtstream.WriteLine("    $txtstream.WriteLine(""}""")")
            txtstream.WriteLine("    $txtstream.WriteLine(""input""")")
            txtstream.WriteLine("    $txtstream.WriteLine(""{""")")
            txtstream.WriteLine("    $txtstream.WriteLine(""    BORDER-RIGHT: #999999 3px solid;""")")
            txtstream.WriteLine("    $txtstream.WriteLine(""    PADDING-RIGHT: 3px;""")")
            txtstream.WriteLine("    $txtstream.WriteLine(""    PADDING-LEFT: 3px;""")")
            txtstream.WriteLine("    $txtstream.WriteLine(""    FONT-WEIGHT: Bold;""")")
            txtstream.WriteLine("    $txtstream.WriteLine(""    PADDING-BOTTOM: 3px;""")")
            txtstream.WriteLine("    $txtstream.WriteLine(""  COLOR: white;""")")
            txtstream.WriteLine("    $txtstream.WriteLine(""    PADDING-TOP: 3px;""")")
            txtstream.WriteLine("    $txtstream.WriteLine(""    BORDER-BOTTOM: #999 1px solid;""")")
            txtstream.WriteLine("    $txtstream.WriteLine(""    BACKGROUND-COLOR: navy;""")")
            txtstream.WriteLine("    $txtstream.WriteLine(""    FONT-FAMILY: font-family: Cambria, serif;""")")
            txtstream.WriteLine("    $txtstream.WriteLine(""    FONT-SIZE: 12px;""")")
            txtstream.WriteLine("    $txtstream.WriteLine(""    text-align: left;""")")
```

```
            txtstream.WriteLine("        $txtstream.WriteLine(""        display: table-
cell;"")")
            txtstream.WriteLine("        $txtstream.WriteLine(""        white-Space:
nowrap;"")")
            txtstream.WriteLine("    $txtstream.WriteLine(""    width: 100%;"")")
            txtstream.WriteLine("    $txtstream.WriteLine(""}"")")
            txtstream.WriteLine("    $txtstream.WriteLine(""h1 {"")")
            txtstream.WriteLine("                $txtstream.WriteLine(""color:
antiquewhite;"")")
            txtstream.WriteLine("    $txtstream.WriteLine(""text-shadow: 1px 1px
1px black;"")")
            txtstream.WriteLine("    $txtstream.WriteLine(""padding: 3px;"")")
            txtstream.WriteLine("                $txtstream.WriteLine(""text-align:
center;"")")
            txtstream.WriteLine("    $txtstream.WriteLine(""box-shadow: in2px
2px 5px rgba(0,0,0,0.5), in-2px -2px 5px rgba(255,255,255,0.5);"")")
            txtstream.WriteLine("    $txtstream.WriteLine(""}"")")
            txtstream.WriteLine("    $txtstream.WriteLine(""</style>"")")

        Case "Customized"

            txtstream.WriteLine("                $txtstream.WriteLine(""<style
type='text/css'>"")")
            txtstream.WriteLine("    $txtstream.WriteLine(""body"")")
            txtstream.WriteLine("    $txtstream.WriteLine(""{"")")
            txtstream.WriteLine("    $txtstream.WriteLine(""    PADDING-RIGHT:
0px;"")")
            txtstream.WriteLine("    $txtstream.WriteLine(""    PADDING-LEFT:
0px;"")")
            txtstream.WriteLine("                $txtstream.WriteLine(""    PADDING-
BOTTOM: 0px;"")")
            txtstream.WriteLine("    $txtstream.WriteLine(""    MARGIN: 0px;"")")
            txtstream.WriteLine("    $txtstream.WriteLine(""    COLOR: #333;"")")
            txtstream.WriteLine("    $txtstream.WriteLine(""    PADDING-TOP:
0px;"")")
            txtstream.WriteLine("    $txtstream.WriteLine(""    FONT-FAMILY:
verdana, arial, helvetica, sans-serif;"")")
            txtstream.WriteLine("    $txtstream.WriteLine(""}"")")
            txtstream.WriteLine("    $txtstream.WriteLine(""Table"")")
            txtstream.WriteLine("    $txtstream.WriteLine(""{"")")
```

```
            txtstream.WriteLine("    $txtstream.WriteLine(""   BORDER-RIGHT:
#999999 1px solid;"")")
            txtstream.WriteLine("    $txtstream.WriteLine(""   PADDING-RIGHT:
1px;"")")
            txtstream.WriteLine("    $txtstream.WriteLine(""   PADDING-LEFT:
1px;"")")
            txtstream.WriteLine("      $txtstream.WriteLine(""      PADDING-
BOTTOM: 1px;"")")
            txtstream.WriteLine("    $txtstream.WriteLine(""   LINE-HEIGHT:
8px;"")")
            txtstream.WriteLine("    $txtstream.WriteLine(""   PADDING-TOP:
1px;"")")
            txtstream.WriteLine("  $txtstream.WriteLine(""  BORDER-BOTTOM:
#999 1px solid;"")")
            txtstream.WriteLine("    $txtstream.WriteLine(""   BACKGROUND-
COLOR: #eeeeee;"")")
            txtstream.WriteLine("                    $txtstream.WriteLine(""
filter:progid:DXImageTransform.Microsoft.Shadow(color='silver',    Direction=135,
Strength=16)"")")
            txtstream.WriteLine("  $txtstream.WriteLine(""}"")")
            txtstream.WriteLine("  $txtstream.WriteLine(""th"")")
            txtstream.WriteLine("  $txtstream.WriteLine(""{"")")
            txtstream.WriteLine("    $txtstream.WriteLine(""   BORDER-RIGHT:
#999999 3px solid;"")")
            txtstream.WriteLine("    $txtstream.WriteLine(""   PADDING-RIGHT:
6px;"")")
            txtstream.WriteLine("    $txtstream.WriteLine(""   PADDING-LEFT:
6px;"")")
            txtstream.WriteLine("    $txtstream.WriteLine(""   FONT-WEIGHT:
Bold;"")")
            txtstream.WriteLine("     $txtstream.WriteLine(""    FONT-SIZE:
14px;"")")
            txtstream.WriteLine("    $txtstream.WriteLine(""   PADDING-
BOTTOM: 6px;"")")
            txtstream.WriteLine("      $txtstream.WriteLine(""     COLOR:
darkred;"")")
            txtstream.WriteLine("    $txtstream.WriteLine(""   LINE-HEIGHT:
14px;"")")
            txtstream.WriteLine("    $txtstream.WriteLine(""   PADDING-TOP:
6px;"")")
```

```
txtstream.WriteLine("          $txtstream.WriteLine(""    BORDER-BOTTOM:
#999 1px solid;"")")
txtstream.WriteLine("          $txtstream.WriteLine(""    BACKGROUND-
COLOR: #eeeeee;"")")
txtstream.WriteLine("          $txtstream.WriteLine(""    FONT-FAMILY:
font-family: Cambria, serif;"")")
txtstream.WriteLine("          $txtstream.WriteLine(""    FONT-SIZE:
12px;"")")
txtstream.WriteLine("          $txtstream.WriteLine(""    text-align:
left;"")")
txtstream.WriteLine("          $txtstream.WriteLine(""    white-Space:
nowrap;"")")
txtstream.WriteLine("          $txtstream.WriteLine(""}"")")
txtstream.WriteLine("          $txtstream.WriteLine("".th"")")
txtstream.WriteLine("          $txtstream.WriteLine(""{"")")
txtstream.WriteLine("          $txtstream.WriteLine(""    BORDER-RIGHT:
#999999 2px solid;"")")
txtstream.WriteLine("          $txtstream.WriteLine(""    PADDING-RIGHT:
6px;"")")
txtstream.WriteLine("          $txtstream.WriteLine(""    PADDING-LEFT:
6px;"")")
txtstream.WriteLine("          $txtstream.WriteLine(""    FONT-WEIGHT:
Bold;"")")
txtstream.WriteLine("          $txtstream.WriteLine(""    PADDING-
BOTTOM: 6px;"")")
txtstream.WriteLine("          $txtstream.WriteLine(""    COLOR: black;"")")
txtstream.WriteLine("          $txtstream.WriteLine(""    PADDING-TOP:
6px;"")")
txtstream.WriteLine("          $txtstream.WriteLine(""    BORDER-BOTTOM:
#999 2px solid;"")")
txtstream.WriteLine("          $txtstream.WriteLine(""    BACKGROUND-
COLOR: #eeeeee;"")")
txtstream.WriteLine("          $txtstream.WriteLine(""    FONT-FAMILY:
font-family: Cambria, serif;"")")
txtstream.WriteLine("          $txtstream.WriteLine(""    FONT-SIZE:
10px;"")")
txtstream.WriteLine("          $txtstream.WriteLine(""    text-align:
right;"")")
txtstream.WriteLine("          $txtstream.WriteLine(""    white-Space:
nowrap;"")")
```

```
        txtstream.WriteLine("   $txtstream.WriteLine(""}""")")
        txtstream.WriteLine("   $txtstream.WriteLine(""td""")")
        txtstream.WriteLine("   $txtstream.WriteLine(""{""")")
        txtstream.WriteLine("   $txtstream.WriteLine(""    BORDER-RIGHT:
#999999 3px solid;""")")
        txtstream.WriteLine("   $txtstream.WriteLine(""    PADDING-RIGHT:
6px;""")")
        txtstream.WriteLine("   $txtstream.WriteLine(""    PADDING-LEFT:
6px;""")")
        txtstream.WriteLine("   $txtstream.WriteLine(""    FONT-WEIGHT:
Normal;""")")
        txtstream.WriteLine("   $txtstream.WriteLine(""    PADDING-
BOTTOM: 6px;""")")
        txtstream.WriteLine("   $txtstream.WriteLine(""   COLOR: navy;""")")
        txtstream.WriteLine("   $txtstream.WriteLine(""    LINE-HEIGHT:
14px;""")")
        txtstream.WriteLine("   $txtstream.WriteLine(""    PADDING-TOP:
6px;""")")
        txtstream.WriteLine("   $txtstream.WriteLine(""   BORDER-BOTTOM:
#999 1px solid;""")")
        txtstream.WriteLine("   $txtstream.WriteLine(""    BACKGROUND-
COLOR: #eeeeee;""")")
        txtstream.WriteLine("   $txtstream.WriteLine(""    FONT-FAMILY:
font-family: Cambria, serif;""")")
        txtstream.WriteLine("   $txtstream.WriteLine(""    FONT-SIZE:
12px;""")")
        txtstream.WriteLine("   $txtstream.WriteLine(""    text-align:
left;""")")
        txtstream.WriteLine("   $txtstream.WriteLine(""    white-Space:
nowrap;""")")
        txtstream.WriteLine("   $txtstream.WriteLine(""}""")")
        txtstream.WriteLine("   $txtstream.WriteLine(""div""")")
        txtstream.WriteLine("   $txtstream.WriteLine(""{""")")
        txtstream.WriteLine("   $txtstream.WriteLine(""    BORDER-RIGHT:
#999999 3px solid;""")")
        txtstream.WriteLine("   $txtstream.WriteLine(""    PADDING-RIGHT:
6px;""")")
        txtstream.WriteLine("   $txtstream.WriteLine(""    PADDING-LEFT:
6px;""")")
```

```
            txtstream.WriteLine("            $txtstream.WriteLine(""    FONT-WEIGHT:
Normal;""")")
            txtstream.WriteLine("            $txtstream.WriteLine(""    PADDING-
BOTTOM: 6px;""")")
            txtstream.WriteLine("    $txtstream.WriteLine(""   COLOR: white;""")")
            txtstream.WriteLine("            $txtstream.WriteLine(""    PADDING-TOP:
6px;""")")
            txtstream.WriteLine("    $txtstream.WriteLine(""   BORDER-BOTTOM:
#999 1px solid;""")")
            txtstream.WriteLine("            $txtstream.WriteLine(""    BACKGROUND-
COLOR: navy;""")")
            txtstream.WriteLine("            $txtstream.WriteLine(""    FONT-FAMILY:
font-family: Cambria, serif;""")")
            txtstream.WriteLine("            $txtstream.WriteLine(""    FONT-SIZE:
10px;""")")
            txtstream.WriteLine("            $txtstream.WriteLine(""    text-align:
left;""")")
            txtstream.WriteLine("            $txtstream.WriteLine(""    white-Space:
nowrap;""")")
            txtstream.WriteLine("    $txtstream.WriteLine(""}""")")
            txtstream.WriteLine("    $txtstream.WriteLine(""span""")")
            txtstream.WriteLine("    $txtstream.WriteLine(""{""")")
            txtstream.WriteLine("    $txtstream.WriteLine(""    BORDER-RIGHT:
#999999 3px solid;""")")
            txtstream.WriteLine("            $txtstream.WriteLine(""    PADDING-RIGHT:
3px;""")")
            txtstream.WriteLine("    $txtstream.WriteLine(""    PADDING-LEFT:
3px;""")")
            txtstream.WriteLine("            $txtstream.WriteLine(""    FONT-WEIGHT:
Normal;""")")
            txtstream.WriteLine("            $txtstream.WriteLine(""    PADDING-
BOTTOM: 3px;""")")
            txtstream.WriteLine("    $txtstream.WriteLine(""   COLOR: white;""")")
            txtstream.WriteLine("            $txtstream.WriteLine(""    PADDING-TOP:
3px;""")")
            txtstream.WriteLine("    $txtstream.WriteLine(""   BORDER-BOTTOM:
#999 1px solid;""")")
            txtstream.WriteLine("            $txtstream.WriteLine(""    BACKGROUND-
COLOR: navy;""")")
```

```
txtstream.WriteLine("    $txtstream.WriteLine(""        FONT-FAMILY:
font-family: Cambria, serif;""")")
txtstream.WriteLine("    $txtstream.WriteLine(""        FONT-SIZE:
10px;""")")
txtstream.WriteLine("    $txtstream.WriteLine(""        text-align:
left;""")")
txtstream.WriteLine("    $txtstream.WriteLine(""        white-Space:
nowrap;""")")
txtstream.WriteLine("    $txtstream.WriteLine(""        display: inline-
block;""")")
txtstream.WriteLine("    $txtstream.WriteLine(""    width: 100%;""")")
txtstream.WriteLine("    $txtstream.WriteLine(""}""")")
txtstream.WriteLine("    $txtstream.WriteLine(""textarea""")")
txtstream.WriteLine("    $txtstream.WriteLine(""{""")")
txtstream.WriteLine("    $txtstream.WriteLine(""        BORDER-RIGHT:
#999999 3px solid;""")")
txtstream.WriteLine("    $txtstream.WriteLine(""        PADDING-RIGHT:
3px;""")")
txtstream.WriteLine("    $txtstream.WriteLine(""        PADDING-LEFT:
3px;""")")
txtstream.WriteLine("    $txtstream.WriteLine(""        FONT-WEIGHT:
Normal;""")")
txtstream.WriteLine("    $txtstream.WriteLine(""        PADDING-
BOTTOM: 3px;""")")
txtstream.WriteLine("    $txtstream.WriteLine(""    COLOR: white;""")")
txtstream.WriteLine("    $txtstream.WriteLine(""        PADDING-TOP:
3px;""")")
txtstream.WriteLine("    $txtstream.WriteLine(""        BORDER-BOTTOM:
#999 1px solid;""")")
txtstream.WriteLine("    $txtstream.WriteLine(""        BACKGROUND-
COLOR: navy;""")")
txtstream.WriteLine("    $txtstream.WriteLine(""        FONT-FAMILY:
font-family: Cambria, serif;""")")
txtstream.WriteLine("    $txtstream.WriteLine(""        FONT-SIZE:
12px;""")")
txtstream.WriteLine("    $txtstream.WriteLine(""        text-align:
left;""")")
txtstream.WriteLine("    $txtstream.WriteLine(""    width: 100%;""")")
txtstream.WriteLine("    $txtstream.WriteLine(""}""")")
txtstream.WriteLine("    $txtstream.WriteLine(""select""")")
```

```
txtstream.WriteLine("   $txtstream.WriteLine(""""{""")")
txtstream.WriteLine("   $txtstream.WriteLine(""""   BORDER-RIGHT:
#999999 1px solid;""")")
txtstream.WriteLine("   $txtstream.WriteLine(""""   PADDING-RIGHT:
1px;""")")
txtstream.WriteLine("   $txtstream.WriteLine(""""   PADDING-LEFT:
1px;""")")
txtstream.WriteLine("   $txtstream.WriteLine(""""   FONT-WEIGHT:
Normal;""")")
txtstream.WriteLine("   $txtstream.WriteLine(""""   PADDING-
BOTTOM: 1px;""")")
txtstream.WriteLine("   $txtstream.WriteLine(""""   COLOR: white;""")")
txtstream.WriteLine("   $txtstream.WriteLine(""""   PADDING-TOP:
1px;""")")
txtstream.WriteLine("   $txtstream.WriteLine(""""   BORDER-BOTTOM:
#999 1px solid;""")")
txtstream.WriteLine("   $txtstream.WriteLine(""""   BACKGROUND-
COLOR: navy;""")")
txtstream.WriteLine("   $txtstream.WriteLine(""""   FONT-FAMILY:
Cambria, serif;""")")
txtstream.WriteLine("   $txtstream.WriteLine(""""   FONT-SIZE:
12px;""")")
txtstream.WriteLine("   $txtstream.WriteLine(""""   text-align:
left;""")")
txtstream.WriteLine("   $txtstream.WriteLine(""""   white-Space:
nowrap;""")")
txtstream.WriteLine("   $txtstream.WriteLine(""""   width: 450px;""")")
txtstream.WriteLine("   $txtstream.WriteLine(""""}""")")
txtstream.WriteLine("   $txtstream.WriteLine(""""select1""")")
txtstream.WriteLine("   $txtstream.WriteLine(""""{""")")
txtstream.WriteLine("   $txtstream.WriteLine(""""   BORDER-RIGHT:
#999999 1px solid;""")")
txtstream.WriteLine("   $txtstream.WriteLine(""""   PADDING-RIGHT:
1px;""")")
txtstream.WriteLine("   $txtstream.WriteLine(""""   PADDING-LEFT:
1px;""")")
txtstream.WriteLine("   $txtstream.WriteLine(""""   FONT-WEIGHT:
Normal;""")")
txtstream.WriteLine("   $txtstream.WriteLine(""""   PADDING-
BOTTOM: 1px;""")")
```

```
        txtstream.WriteLine("    $txtstream.WriteLine(""    COLOR: white;"")")
        txtstream.WriteLine("      $txtstream.WriteLine(""      PADDING-TOP:
1px;"")")
        txtstream.WriteLine("     $txtstream.WriteLine(""    BORDER-BOTTOM:
#999 1px solid;"")")
        txtstream.WriteLine("     $txtstream.WriteLine(""     BACKGROUND-
COLOR: navy;"")")
        txtstream.WriteLine("     $txtstream.WriteLine(""     FONT-FAMILY:
Cambria, serif;"")")
        txtstream.WriteLine("      $txtstream.WriteLine(""      FONT-SIZE:
12px;"")")
        txtstream.WriteLine("      $txtstream.WriteLine(""      text-align:
left;"")")
        txtstream.WriteLine("      $txtstream.WriteLine(""      white-Space:
nowrap;"")")
        txtstream.WriteLine("    $txtstream.WriteLine(""    width: 450px;"")")
        txtstream.WriteLine("    $txtstream.WriteLine(""}"")")
        txtstream.WriteLine("    $txtstream.WriteLine(""select2"")")
        txtstream.WriteLine("    $txtstream.WriteLine(""{"")")
        txtstream.WriteLine("     $txtstream.WriteLine(""     BORDER-RIGHT:
#999999 1px solid;"")")
        txtstream.WriteLine("     $txtstream.WriteLine(""     PADDING-RIGHT:
1px;"")")
        txtstream.WriteLine("     $txtstream.WriteLine(""     PADDING-LEFT:
1px;"")")
        txtstream.WriteLine("     $txtstream.WriteLine(""     FONT-WEIGHT:
Normal;"")")
        txtstream.WriteLine("      $txtstream.WriteLine(""      PADDING-
BOTTOM: 1px;"")")
        txtstream.WriteLine("    $txtstream.WriteLine(""    COLOR: white;"")")
        txtstream.WriteLine("      $txtstream.WriteLine(""      PADDING-TOP:
1px;"")")
        txtstream.WriteLine("     $txtstream.WriteLine(""    BORDER-BOTTOM:
#999 1px solid;"")")
        txtstream.WriteLine("     $txtstream.WriteLine(""     BACKGROUND-
COLOR: navy;"")")
        txtstream.WriteLine("     $txtstream.WriteLine(""     FONT-FAMILY:
Cambria, serif;"")")
        txtstream.WriteLine("      $txtstream.WriteLine(""      FONT-SIZE:
12px;"")")
```

```
txtstream.WriteLine("$txtstream.WriteLine(""        text-align: left;""")")
txtstream.WriteLine("$txtstream.WriteLine(""        white-Space: nowrap;""")")
txtstream.WriteLine("$txtstream.WriteLine(""    width: 450px;""")")
txtstream.WriteLine("$txtstream.WriteLine(""}""")")
txtstream.WriteLine("$txtstream.WriteLine(""select3""")")
txtstream.WriteLine("$txtstream.WriteLine(""{""")")
txtstream.WriteLine("$txtstream.WriteLine(""        BORDER-RIGHT: #999999 1px solid;""")")
txtstream.WriteLine("$txtstream.WriteLine(""        PADDING-RIGHT: 1px;""")")
txtstream.WriteLine("$txtstream.WriteLine(""        PADDING-LEFT: 1px;""")")
txtstream.WriteLine("$txtstream.WriteLine(""        FONT-WEIGHT: Normal;""")")
txtstream.WriteLine("$txtstream.WriteLine(""        PADDING-BOTTOM: 1px;""")")
txtstream.WriteLine("$txtstream.WriteLine(""    COLOR: white;""")")
txtstream.WriteLine("$txtstream.WriteLine(""        PADDING-TOP: 1px;""")")
txtstream.WriteLine("$txtstream.WriteLine(""        BORDER-BOTTOM: #999 1px solid;""")")
txtstream.WriteLine("$txtstream.WriteLine(""        BACKGROUND-COLOR: navy;""")")
txtstream.WriteLine("$txtstream.WriteLine(""        FONT-FAMILY: Cambria, serif;""")")
txtstream.WriteLine("$txtstream.WriteLine(""        FONT-SIZE: 12px;""")")
txtstream.WriteLine("$txtstream.WriteLine(""        text-align: left;""")")
txtstream.WriteLine("$txtstream.WriteLine(""        white-Space: nowrap;""")")
txtstream.WriteLine("$txtstream.WriteLine(""    width: 100px;""")")
txtstream.WriteLine("$txtstream.WriteLine(""}""")")
txtstream.WriteLine("$txtstream.WriteLine(""select4""")")
txtstream.WriteLine("$txtstream.WriteLine(""{""")")
txtstream.WriteLine("$txtstream.WriteLine(""        BORDER-RIGHT: #999999 1px solid;""")")
```

```
            txtstream.WriteLine("    $txtstream.WriteLine(""    PADDING-RIGHT: 1px;""")")
            txtstream.WriteLine("    $txtstream.WriteLine(""    PADDING-LEFT: 1px;""")")
            txtstream.WriteLine("    $txtstream.WriteLine(""    FONT-WEIGHT: Normal;""")")
            txtstream.WriteLine("    $txtstream.WriteLine(""    PADDING-BOTTOM: 1px;""")")
            txtstream.WriteLine("    $txtstream.WriteLine(""    COLOR: white;""")")
            txtstream.WriteLine("    $txtstream.WriteLine(""    PADDING-TOP: 1px;""")")
            txtstream.WriteLine("    $txtstream.WriteLine(""    BORDER-BOTTOM: #999 1px solid;""")")
            txtstream.WriteLine("    $txtstream.WriteLine(""    BACKGROUND-COLOR: navy;""")")
            txtstream.WriteLine("    $txtstream.WriteLine(""    FONT-FAMILY: Cambria, serif;""")")
            txtstream.WriteLine("    $txtstream.WriteLine(""    FONT-SIZE: 12px;""")")
            txtstream.WriteLine("    $txtstream.WriteLine(""    text-align: left;""")")
            txtstream.WriteLine("    $txtstream.WriteLine(""    white-Space: nowrap;""")")
            txtstream.WriteLine("    $txtstream.WriteLine(""    width: 254px;""")")
            txtstream.WriteLine("    $txtstream.WriteLine(""}""")")
            txtstream.WriteLine("    $txtstream.WriteLine(""input""")")
            txtstream.WriteLine("    $txtstream.WriteLine(""{""")")
            txtstream.WriteLine("    $txtstream.WriteLine(""    BORDER-RIGHT: #999999 3px solid;""")")
            txtstream.WriteLine("    $txtstream.WriteLine(""    PADDING-RIGHT: 3px;""")")
            txtstream.WriteLine("    $txtstream.WriteLine(""    PADDING-LEFT: 3px;""")")
            txtstream.WriteLine("    $txtstream.WriteLine(""    FONT-WEIGHT: Bold;""")")
            txtstream.WriteLine("    $txtstream.WriteLine(""    PADDING-BOTTOM: 3px;""")")
            txtstream.WriteLine("    $txtstream.WriteLine(""    COLOR: white;""")")
            txtstream.WriteLine("    $txtstream.WriteLine(""    PADDING-TOP: 3px;""")")
```

```
            txtstream.WriteLine("    $txtstream.WriteLine(""    BORDER-BOTTOM:
#999 1px solid;"")")
            txtstream.WriteLine("    $txtstream.WriteLine(""    BACKGROUND-
COLOR: navy;"")")
            txtstream.WriteLine("    $txtstream.WriteLine(""    FONT-FAMILY:
font-family: Cambria, serif;"")")
            txtstream.WriteLine("    $txtstream.WriteLine(""    FONT-SIZE:
12px;"")")
            txtstream.WriteLine("    $txtstream.WriteLine(""    text-align:
left;"")")
            txtstream.WriteLine("    $txtstream.WriteLine(""    display: table-
cell;"")")
            txtstream.WriteLine("    $txtstream.WriteLine(""    white-Space:
nowrap;"")")
            txtstream.WriteLine("    $txtstream.WriteLine(""    width: 100%;"")")
            txtstream.WriteLine("    $txtstream.WriteLine(""}"")")
            txtstream.WriteLine("    $txtstream.WriteLine(""</style>"")")

        End Select

    End Sub

    </script>

    </body>
    </html>
```

Above this line is where it ends.

Merry Christmas!